E-Government in Kazakhstan

IØ128959

When it comes to analyzing the phenomenon of digital government, the over-whelming focus is on the most developed nations in the world, and Western countries in particular. However, Kazakhstan, a post-totalitarian country, has also proved to be successful in the development of e-government.

This book analyzes e-government development in Kazakhstan from a multitude of dimensions, including, but not limited to, political, social, economic and technological platforms. It examines the adoption of a wide range of technology-driven public sector projects and identifies the key drivers, challenges, regulation policies and stakeholders of e-government reforms in this transitional society. Taking into account recent changes in governance, such as the development of mobile government, the rise of civic engagement and the open data-driven movement, and the overall formal progress of the e-government project, this book addresses the emergence of new challenges and concerns associated with the advancement of the e-government concept. Furthermore, it suggests that a universal framework can be applied when investigating e-government projects in the developing world.

Offering a wide range of practical recommendations on how to overcome the problems associated with e-government development, this book will be a valuable resource for anyone wishing to improve their understanding of the multidimensional nature of e-government. It will also be of key interest to academics studying Political Science, Development Studies, Public Policy and Central Asian Studies.

Maxat Kassen is Associate Professor at the Eurasian Humanitarian Institute, Kazakhstan.

Routledge Advances in Central Asian Studies

For a full list of titles in this series, please visit www.routledge.com/Routledge-Advances-in-Central-Asian-Studies/book-series/RACAS

E-Government in Kazakhstan

A case study of multidimensional phenomena

Maxat Kassen

Routledge
Taylor & Francis Group

LONDON AND NEW YORK

First published 2017 by Routledge

2 Park Square, Milton Park, Abingdon, Oxon, OX14 4RN
605 Third Avenue, New York, NY 10017

Routledge is an imprint of the Taylor & Francis Group, an informa business

First issued in paperback 2020

British Library Cataloguing in Publication Data
A catalogue record for this book is available from the British Library

Library of Congress Cataloging-in-Publication Data
A catalog record for this book has been requested

ISBN: 978-1-138-22070-6 (hbk)
ISBN: 978-0-367-78820-9 (pbk)

Typeset in Times New Roman
by Apex CoVantage, LLC

Contents

Figures

Tables

About the author

Maxat Kassen is a political scientist and a docent teaching students in the Eurasian Humanitarian Institute in Astana, Kazakhstan. He is a former head of foreign information service in the National Information Agency – Kazinform (2003–2004). He is also a former Fulbright Visiting Scholar at the University of Illinois at Chicago (2011–2012) and fellow of the Annenberg-Oxford Summer Institute at the University of Oxford (2011). His research focuses on studying the impact of new information technologies on domestic politics and international relations, especially in analyzing the e-government phenomenon, globalization of the open data movement and transformation of the political communication channels. He has several works on digital politics and use of e-government technologies published in prestigious international high-impact factor academic journals.

Foreword

In academic and professional literature, the phenomenon of digital government is usually analyzed in the context of the most developed and democratic nations of the world with a majority of case studies focused on Western countries, forgetting that it is a global trend. In contrast to the traditional tendencies in literature, the author of this book investigates the phenomena in an unusual context, resorting to the case study of a typical emerging and post-totalitarian country such as Kazakhstan and focusing on the analysis of the key drivers and challenges in the diffusion of the e-government movement to answer the ultimate question: whether it is harnessed by the members of civil society to promote civic engagement and new political communication.

In general, the results of the case study research presented in this book are useful as analytical material by providing a detailed review of various e-government, open data and e-participation projects; investigating political, economic, social and institutional challenges associated with their development; and offering a wide range of practical recommendations on how to overcome them, providing an interesting, unique and rich empirical basis for policy makers and practitioners, political scientists and journalists, as well as students of public administration and all those who seek to understand better an amazing multidimensional nature of e-government.

.

1 Methodology of case study research

The primary purpose of the chapter is to outline the investigation framework of the research to help establish the correct methodological foundation of the analysis, which will mostly be based on a case study of the e-government development in Kazakhstan in its various dimensions and institutional levels, including but not limited to political, social, economic and technological ones; first, by setting the research questions and shaping the investigation skeleton of the study, determining the key areas of concentration and choosing the appropriate research methods as well as providing some generalizations on expected findings and outcomes of the research.

Introduction: e-government as a multidimensional political phenomenon

The obvious and foremost step in starting any scientific effort is to understand first the subject of the investigation itself and then provide its definition, which would presumably help to build a stable theoretical foundation to further the research. However, in the case of e-government studies, it is not an easy task. Asking a simple question such as, "What is e-government really?" might be tricky and perplexing yet surprisingly heuristic and didactic because it could generate a plethora of answers and explanations from academics in almost any science and practitioners from almost any country or area of expertise. Each perspective, in this respect, will be fairly valid and logically sound in providing definitions that are practice based and developed on generalizations of myriad insightful e-government stories, making the phenomenon an interesting area to investigate and explore. Any achievements in the digital arena indirectly affect the development of the concept in its various aspects whether open data or e-participation, digital political communication or electoral campaigns, civic engagement or even international relations, making the paradigm extremely multidimensional and fruitful in generating new domains for research in nearly any discipline.

The apparent *reincarnative* nature of the e-government academic paradigm, reflected in the emergence of new dimensions of the concept – such as open government, e-government 2.0 and even e-government 3.0, mobile government, interactive government, smart government, we-government, open data-driven local government, connected government, online government, etc. – has created a new direction in e-government studies that studies the research on e-government itself, generating an unprecedented amount of knowledge and expertise in an age-long attempt to comprehend the incomprehensible universe of the e-government phenomenon and its related use of information and communication technologies (ICT) in public sector reforms. Perhaps, when it comes to e-government-related areas whether in industry or agriculture, business or transportation, public administration or politics, taking into account its multidimensional and, most important, ever-changing nature, we should never stop asking *what it really is*. This is what makes the topic so amazingly attractive, engaging and promising to explore.

In this respect, in an enriching endeavor to understand the phenomenon of e-government in Kazakhstan, the author of this book will apply a multidimensional approach, especially in analyzing the nuances of political communication and socioeconomic relationships that emerge in e-government projects and networks. The generated vertical and peer-to-peer communication channels in these networks are of special interest in the research because generalizations in this area could provide a fruitful foundation for further investigations into other dimensions of the phenomenon. In this respect, e-government is generally understood as an ICT-driven public sector project aimed at providing various electronic services (e-services) to citizens, nongovernmental organizations (NGOs), developers, businesses, media and other government agencies, which encompasses a wide variety of digital platforms and projects realized both at the national and local levels of governance with or without participation of the civil society.

E-government in Kazakhstan: the research background

There is a shortage of publications on the development of e-government in Kazakhstan. In this regard, among the most prominent works by scientists who have investigated the topic are publications by Bhuiyan, Janenova and Kassen, namely, "E-Government in Kazakhstan: Challenges and Its Role to Development" (Bhuiyan, 2010), "Trajectories of E-Government Implementation for Public Sector Service Delivery in Kazakhstan" (Bhuiyan, 2011), "E-Government in Kazakhstan: Challenges for a Transitional Country" (Janenova, 2010), "E-Government in Kazakhstan: Realization and Prospects" (Kassen, 2010) and "Understanding Systems of e-Government:

e-Federalism and e-Centralism in the United States and Kazakhstan" (Kassen, 2015). Among other publications that partly analyzed the topic, it is also necessary to note the works by Åström et al. and Knox "Understanding the rise of e-participation in non-democracies: Domestic and international factors" (Åström et al., 2012) and "Kazakhstan: modernizing government in the context of political inertia" (Knox, 2008).

Although these publications provide a comprehensive and critical analysis of developments in the e-government sphere from various perspectives, most of them were published several years ago and, therefore, do not reflect in a holistic and comprehensive manner the recent changes in the promotion of the concept in Kazakhstan such as the development of mobile government, the rise of civic engagement and open data-driven movement and overall progress of the project in various dimensions reflected in the dramatic promotion of the country in global e-government ratings in 2012, 2014 and 2016, which is ripe for analysis. Likewise, the emergence of new challenges and concerns associated with the advancement of the e-government concept in new economic and political environments demands further investigations in these areas of the phenomenon, too.

Building the framework for case study research

Taking into account the need for new research on e-government in Kazakhstan, especially in investigating various political and socioeconomic implications of the latest developments and trends in the sphere and the changeable and unpredictable nature of the ICT-driven public sector reforms, it seems logical to apply a more holistic and comprehensive approach in studying the phenomenon based on a new set of investigation topics, associated research questions and methodology.

Setting the research agenda

Five research questions shape the framework of the case study in this book. Each chapter of the analyzes the following research topics, correspondingly:

1   What is the country's readiness in various areas to adopt the e-government projects (e.g. in political and social fields, economy, regional development, ICT sphere and Internet governance, foreign policy, mass media development, etc.)? More important, what are the key drivers and barriers of e-government development in Kazakhstan?

2   What is the history of e-government development in Kazakhstan? What are the key e-government projects? What kind of strategies has been applied to promote them? What regulatory acts have been adopted

to support the e-government policies? Who have been the key decision makers in the sphere?
3   What new e-government projects have been realized recently in Kazakhstan? What is the public value of the projects?
4   How does the realization of the open government concept promote digital democracy in Kazakhstan?
5   What are the drivers and challenges of the e-participation and civic engagement movement in Kazakhstan?

Methods of analysis and expected results

In choosing the right methodology of research, it is important to build a framework that could help to specify potential investigation topics, identify a set of appropriate tools of the analysis and even speculate on expected findings. In this respect, a case study seems to be the best research strategy, because it allows one to build and test hypotheses (Eisenhardt, 1989) as well as analyze the topic in all of its diversity (Chen et al., 2006) in one particular country as a current multidimensional political and socioeconomic process (Yin, 2013). The case study in e-government research is probably one of the most interesting investigation methods because it allows us to apply *a scattergun approach* (see figure 1.1) with a combination of various methods of analysis such as:

1   *a context analysis* in analyzing the country background and its implications for the development of e-government as a multidimensional phenomenon, which could be helpful in predicting the adoption of the ICT-driven innovations in the public sector. In this regard, the author of the book will try to analyze the implications of contexts such as political system, national economy, regional development, geography of the country, the information and communication sector, mass media, and foreign policy on the development of e-government;
2   *a retrospective analysis,* which could be helpful in identifying the key periods of the e-government development in Kazakhstan. In this regard, the topic will be analyzed from four, presumably different, viewpoints: *from the perspective of the key e-government projects and platforms,* which contributed to the diffusion of the concept in Kazakhstan*; from the perspective of the analysis of the adopted regulatory acts and laws; from the perspective of key e-government stakeholders* which activities are usually correlated with key directions of the strategic programs and political statements in the sphere; and, finally, *from the international perspective* reflected in the overall progress of e-government in various international ratings and contests, information

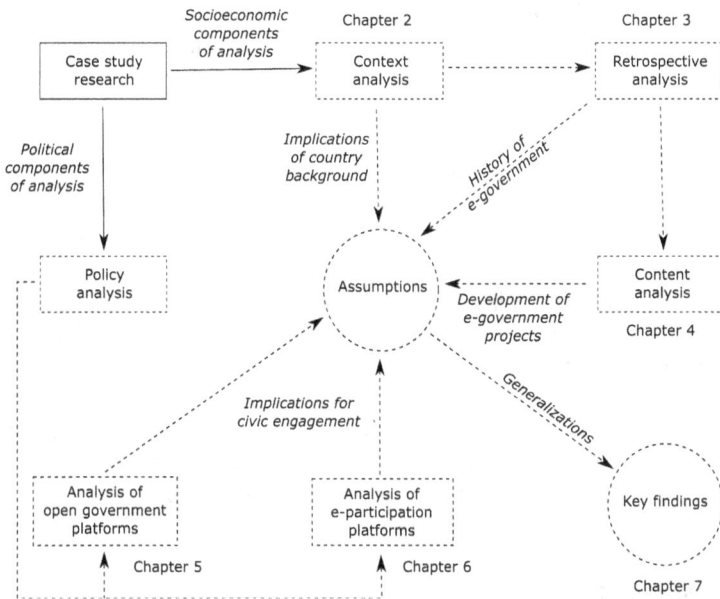

Figure 1.1 Building the framework for the case study research on e-government in Kazakhstan

Source: own illustration

which is usually provided by international organizations and agencies such as the United Nations and the World Bank in their biennial global surveys;

3   *a content analysis*, which might be used in the analysis of *the e-government projects* to identify the most popular interactive services, social media channels, startups and platforms, understand the realization strategies and tactics from the perspectives of various stakeholders (e.g. public agencies, citizens, businesses, NGOs, media, ICT developers, etc.);

4   *a policy analysis* which could be extremely helpful in analyzing critically *the open government and e-participation phenomenon* in its close relationship to the political contexts of the ICT-driven public sector reforms, political decisions made and motives, and, especially in understanding the *public value* of the open data initiatives aimed at the promotion of the e-participation and civic engagement platforms by the national authorities in the area. In this regard, the e-government policies will be analyzed from two perspectives: first, from the benefits of the ICT-driven reforms in *public administration* and, second, from the perspective of benefits of the e-government reforms *in the political*

domain, especially in analyzing the public value of related concepts such as open government, civic engagement, political communication, and its impact on diffusion of digital democracy in Kazakhstan.

The key sources of data and information for analysis

The study is mostly based on the analysis of data from various international organizations and statistical agencies in the sphere. In this regard, the data will be investigated from the following perspectives: *the analysis of the related regulatory acts*, which also will be subdivided, for example, in accordance with a principle of administrative division (e.g. e-government legislation at the national and local levels of public administration) and with relevance to the e-government area (e.g. direct and indirect influence on the sphere, etc.); *analysis of the key sources for statistical data*, which will be then subdivided in accordance with a geographical principle (e.g. statistics at the global, national and local levels) and authority of the source (e.g. official data, i.e. provided by government, and unofficial data, which could be provided by NGOs, universities and private ICT corporations); *analysis of the e-government portals and platforms*, which, in turn, will be subdivided in accordance with the type of e-government platforms (e.g. ordinary desktop and mobile versions of the portals), in accordance with the type of e-government services (e.g. platforms that provide information, interactive or transactional e-services); in accordance with the target audiences (e.g. platforms designed for citizens, businesses or other government agencies) and in accordance with the authority of e-government platforms (e.g. projects created by government or independent players such NGOs, independent ICT developers, technically savvy citizens, etc.); and, finally, *analysis of other sources of data and information* (e.g. mass media, statistics from online search machines, web counters, official accounts in social media, etc.).

References

Åström, J., Karlsson, M., Linde, J., & Pirannejad, A. (2012). Understanding the rise of e-participation in non-democracies: Domestic and international factors. *Government Information Quarterly*, *29*(2), 142–150.

Bhuiyan, S. H. (2010). E-government in Kazakhstan: Challenges and its role to development. *Public Organization Review*, *10*(1), 31–47.

Bhuiyan, S. H. (2011). Trajectories of e-government implementation for public sector service delivery in Kazakhstan. *International Journal of Public Administration*, *34*(9), 604–615.

Chen, Y. N., Chen, H. M., Huang, W., & Ching, R. K. (2006). E-government strategies in developed and developing countries: An implementation framework and case study. *Journal of Global Information Management*, *14*(1), 23–46.

Eisenhardt, K. M. (1989). Building theories from case study research. *Academy of Management Review*, *14*(4), 532–550.

Janenova, S. (2010). E-Government in Kazakhstan: Challenges for a transitional country. In *18th NISPAcee Annual Conference "Public Administration in Times of Crisis"* (pp. 12–14). Warsaw, Poland.

Kassen, M. (2010). *E-Government in Kazakhstan: Realization and prospects*, 6. Carbondale: Open SIUC, Southern Illinois University. http://opensiuc.lib.siu.edu/pnconfs_2010/6/

Kassen, M. (2015). *Understanding systems of e-Government: E-Federalism and e-Centralism in the United States and Kazakhstan*. Lanham, MD: Lexington Books.

Knox, C. (2008). Kazakhstan: Modernizing government in the context of political inertia. *International Review of Administrative Sciences*, *74*(3), 477–496.

Yin, R. K. (2013). *Case study research: Design and methods*. Thousand Oaks, CA: Sage Publications.

2 The country context analysis of Kazakhstan

Implications for e-government

This chapter is dedicated to the country context analysis of the political and socioeconomic development of Kazakhstan in various areas from the perspective of its indirect impact on the promotion of e-government, for example, such as the implications of its geography and territorial division, history of the country, its political and social systems, public administration, economy, telecommunication industry, mass media, civil society and foreign policy in order to identify the challenges and promises of the country readiness to realize e-government in all its diversity.

The framework for the country context analysis

Taking into account the fact that e-government is a multidimensional political phenomenon whose development is indirectly affected by an extremely wide range of background factors and variables, it is important to develop a research framework for the country context analysis that helps to identify the key features of the e-government environments in various spheres and analyze how they affect the development of the ICT-driven public sector reforms – i.e. understand the motivations, key challenges and promises to harness the potential of the technology from these perspectives.

The multidimensional contexts of e-government

The geography: being transcontinentally landlocked

Looking at the global map, one can easily notice that geographically Kazakhstan is the largest landlocked country in the world, which is at the center of a huge continent called Eurasia – i.e. at the intersection of major transportation, telecommunication and trade routes that connect Asia and Europe. In terms of the area, Kazakhstan is the ninth largest country in the world, with vast but sparsely populated territories characterized by deserts and semi-desert steppes. This fact makes the task of e-government realization logistically challenging, because the large area of the country also implies a higher cost of infrastructure creation, especially in building the telecommunication lines and networks in remote rural areas, which are necessary for successful implementation of various ICT-driven public sector reforms, and partly explains the interest of the nation in the development of satellite technologies (Warf, 2013), which could potentially decrease the price of telecommunication services.

Administratively, the territory of the country is subdivided into fourteen provinces or regions (*oblys* in Kazakh or *oblystar* in plural form) and two major cities, Almaty and Astana, both of which have special status as the largest megalopolis and the capital city, respectively. However, politically these regions do not enjoy autonomy from the center, since Kazakhstan is a unitary state with a strong structure of power relationships between the capital city and regional authorities. In this regard, hypothetically, the unique unitary nature of the administrative and territorial division of the country makes the task of e-government promotion much easier because the development of the projects is usually initiated and implemented mostly by the central government agencies while the regional projects in the sphere are regarded as merely administrative units of the single e-government project, which is realized at the national level. In this respect, e-government is also considered as a platform that allows citizens to receive almost all public e-services interactively from one venue regardless of their location. Taking into account that people have to travel long distances to receive one paper document from national and sometimes even from local authorities, the large territory of the country and lack of good roads and transportation provide a huge economic motivation to develop e-government that could presumably help to make people's lives much easier by providing the most popular public services in an electronic format. This is, probably, one of the most important implications of the country's geography on the development of the ICT-driven public sector reforms.

Key features of the geography

1   Large territory of the country
2   Relatively small population
3   Unitary structure of the territorial division

Implications for e-government

CHALLENGES

The large and sparsely populated territory of the country implies higher logistical costs for the infrastructure, especially in building and maintaining national telecommunication systems and networks, which is a basic requirement for the normal functioning of e-government projects.

One of the paradoxical implications of the country's geography is that the unitary character of its administrative and territorial division into regions and counties (*audandar* in Kazakh), with a strong central position, theoretically allows the public decision makers to promote more effectively a single e-government policy.

The national history: overcoming the gloomy moments of the past

Kazakhstan has an ancient and rich history that dates back to the time of the Huns. For many centuries, its territory both politically and administratively has been regarded as one of the most important centers of the Turkic World and Golden Horde. Since its foundation in the fifteenth century as a monarchy and up to the middle of the nineteenth century, when it was finally conquered by the Russian Empire, the Kazakh Khanate had played an important role as a cultural and economic bridge between Europe and Asia. The twentieth century was, probably, one of the most tragic periods in the history of Kazakhstan. The forced collectivization (Olcott, 1981), initiated in early 1930s by the Soviet authorities, destroyed the traditional well-functioning nomadic way of life which led to unprecedented famine among Kazakhs that was responsible for millions of lives (Pianciola, 2001; Ohayon, 2013). The cruel policy of collectivization and concurrent relentless political repressions against its political, aristocratic and intellectual elite, aimed at eliminating any thought of national independence and creating a pandemic sense of fear of impending arrests and apprehension, not only severely decreased the population of the nation but also dramatically changed the public mindset of the people, leaving virtually no chance for the development of free thought, critical or democratic mentality crucial for the emergence of the civil society. The following political deportations and economic immigration of millions of people from other parts of the Soviet Union to Kazakhstan significantly changed the ethnic composition of the country, while the ill-conceived policy of industrialization led to catastrophic consequences for nature, creating multiple environmental issues across the country such as the radioactive pollution near the Semipalatinsk Nuclear Testing Site (Takada et al., 1999; Simon, Baverstock & Lindholm, 2003), the desiccation of the Aral Sea (Micklin, 2007), chemical pollution from the Baikonur space-launch complex (Carlsen et al., 2010; Abdrazak & Musa, 2015), etc.

Speaking about the implications of national history on the development of e-government, it is interesting to mention that the independence of Kazakhstan, declared after the collapse of the Soviet Union in 1991, revived people's interest in their historical past (Diener, 2002), culture and language. In this regard, the emergence of various e-government projects such as the e-history (The e-history project, 2015) and e-culture projects (The e-culture project, 2015) as part of the e-government realization policy provides a unique opportunity to preserve and keep in historical archives for future generations (see figure 2.1).

The digitalization of stockpiles of once-classified documents and archival files from the country's tragic past could be one of the promising directions of the e-government policy, while various civic engagement projects that might be created around the open data-driven movements could help the national and local authorities to better solve the consequences of the ecological catastrophes together with the environmental NGOs and research centers. In fact, the renaissance in political activity of people in Kazakhstan in the late 1980s during the Perestroika times could be associated with the

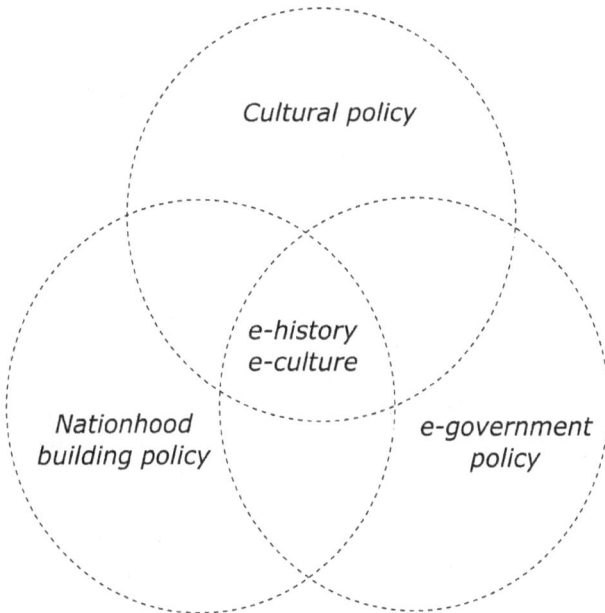

Figure 2.1 The intersections of the cultural, nationhood-building and e-government policies in Kazakhstan

Source: own illustration

rise of various environmental movements at that time, some of which later transformed into political parties and organizations such as the Nevada-Semey Movement (Brown, 1990), Tabigat, etc.

Key features of the national history

1   Ancient history and rich culture
2   Oppressive and tragic past
3   Consequences of environmental pollution

Implications for e-government

CHALLENGES

The traditional public mindset based on the historical memory of the oppressive past and lack of democratic traditions in building a civil society could provide obstacles in developing the civic engagement component of e-government.

PROMISES

People are beginning to display an interest in the ancient and rich history of the country, which could be used in the development of various e-government projects and, generally, is conducive for the emergence of independent peer-to-peer e-participation platforms in the sphere.

The political system: a controversial paradox

The political system of Kazakhstan has a somewhat two-fold and controversial character. On the one hand, it has all modern political institutions such as the separation of powers and declared multiparty system in the constitution, but on the other hand, the existence of many presumably democratic institutions is a mere formality since they do not reflect the hidden political processes in the system with their own sets of values, unwritten rules and key players. Officially, Kazakhstan is a strong presidential republic where the role of the head of state is crucial in many spheres since he determines the domestic and foreign policy of the country, as well as appoints the prime minister and de facto forms the cabinet. In this regard, it is the national government that is a focal point of all state-run projects and initiatives in public administration, including the e-government sphere, which makes the implementation of many projects in the sphere much easier than in countries with more decentralized structures of government. In addition, institutionally, the political power belongs to a ruling Nur Otan party (Isaacs, 2011). Defined by Bader (2011) as "hegemonic" or a "super party" by Bowyer (2008), it has overwhelming partisan control at the lower houses of the national parliament – Mazhilis. Therefore, almost all members of the executive branch of power both at the national and local levels of government are members of this political organization.

In this regard, the structure of power relationships within the unitary government is usually characterized by a strong top-down mechanism of administrative control and organization, which, along with a single partisanship, is at first look conducive to the development of a single national e-government project (Kassen, 2015), since it is easier to politically pursue and organizationally implement the ICT-driven public sector reforms with an advantageous centralized mechanism of administrative control (Stier, 2015) and financing, relying juridically on a single legislation in the area and technologically using universal e-government platforms and databases whether it is at the national or local levels. However, it also creates an environment of ubiquitous servile flattery and traditions of straightforward and unquestioning fulfillment among members of the political and administrative systems due to a strict top-down machine of decision making, which dramatically increases the chances of mistakes and fallacies. The common sense says that some constructive criticism of the e-government politics and discretion in the decision-making processes might be beneficial for overall successful and sustainable future development.

Key features of the political system

1 Strong presidential system of government
2 Single partisanship in legislative and executive branches of power both at the national and local levels
3 Top-down decision-making mechanism

Implications for e-government

CHALLENGES

The strong top-down structure of power relationships existing in the political system discourages a wholesome atmosphere of self-criticism and discretion, which is crucial for the development of various e-government projects in the modern sense – e.g. in promoting e-participation, peer-to-peer and civic engagement platforms.

PROMISES

Paradoxically, the high level of political centralization and administrative hierarchy in the system could be extremely efficient in the short term for the promotion of the single e-government project because of speedier decision-making processes and direct political control and scrutiny from the center.

The social system: challenges and promises of diversity

Although the population of Kazakhstan is about 17 million people, which is relatively small taking into account the size of its territory, from the perspective of its social composition, it is one of the most socially and ethnically diverse societies in the world. Many years of deportations (Polian, 2004) and migrations of various ethnic (Kendirbaeva, 1997) and religious groups and even whole nations to Kazakhstan during the Soviet repressions from 1930 to the 1950s have resulted in the creation of a cosmopolitan society in this transcontinental country. One of the consequences of the policy is the existence of bilingual communities – Kazakh and Russian ones; all public documents such as laws and other legal acts as well as public information and content on governmental portals and systems are provided in those two languages. As a result, one of the important aspects in the development of the public e-government portals is the necessity to translate all documents to meet the requirements of the law which, in some cases, requires a staff of bilingual specialists or even professional translators in many government agencies due to a high volume of the government data sets and importance of the translated documents.

The baby boom phenomenon that Kazakhstan is experiencing today increases pressure on the available pool of kindergartens and schools and demand for new apartments for the growing number of young families and new citizens. The shortage of available and affordable housing in the market creates a huge pressure in the sphere and the issue is widely regarded as one of the most urgent social problems. In this regard, public e-services that address the challenge – for example, the national public housing project which helps people to save money and receive later mortgages on easy terms (Zhilstroysberbank Project, 2015) – are in great demand and popular among citizens today. In order to ensure the increased transparency of government activity in the distribution of public housing, the portal that represents this project is closely synchronized with the work of the e-government system and operates on the same principle. For instance, by creating a special online account, citizens could submit and track their e-applications for the discounted public housing that is being built in various regions of the country. In this regard, the unprecedented growth of the capital city in the last two decades explains the fact that Astana, whose population has increased fourfold due to the internal migration from other regions, is a notorious example of the shortages in housing in the country as a whole which, to some extent, explains the recent popularity of e-services related to the housing sphere (The E-Government of Kazakhstan, 2015) and might be regarded as one of the implications of the demographics on the development of the concept in Kazakhstan. In this respect, civic engagement and increased e-participation that arguably becomes possible thanks to the launch of independent open data-driven and wiki-based projects might be promising, too.

Key features of the social system

1 Ethnically and religiously diverse society
2 Bilingual communities
3 Growing population and domestic hyper migration

Implications for e-government

CHALLENGES

The existence of the bilingual communities requires additional human and financial resources to provide all e-government services in two languages. The simultaneous translation of large volumes of documents and data sets requires bilingual professionals in the public administration systems, increasing the overall operational cost of the e-government projects.

PROMISES

The growing number of citizens because of the high birth rate and immigration creates a favorable environment for the development of related e-services, including those that are created by citizens themselves through civic engagement, that presumably could help address social issues such as a deficit of information on affordable public housing in the market and places in kindergartens, distribution of public housing and other social benefits among citizens.

The public administration system: how to reform bureaucracy?

The public administration system of Kazakhstan is one of the sectors of the national economy that often undergoes various structural reorganizations officially aimed at making the civil service both professional and depoliticized, yet reaching modest results in either way (Emrich-Bakenova, 2009).

One of the primary reasons for the reforms was a number of administrative changes that the country had to go through since 1991 when it gained independence (Perlman & Gleason, 2007). In this regard, since many institutions of public administration inherited at that time from the Soviet past no longer functioned properly because of new political realities and the inability of the old bureaucratic machine to answer new challenges in the economy, the sphere became one of the first playgrounds to experiment with a number of public sector reforms with varying success. Perhaps, one of the fundamental changes has affected the structure of the public administration system, since all public servants are now divided into two different categories, each with its own regulations and rules of conduct and duties – the class of political public servants, which consists of about several hundred people and the class of so-called administrative public servants – i.e. the layer that consists of those who represent an army of government agents. According to Alikhan Baymenov, head of the Civil Service Agency of Kazakhstan, the government organization that supervises the development of the public administration system, in 2014 the number of civil servants was approximately 97,000 people, of which only 9,000 worked at central government agencies (The Center of Government Efficiency Evaluation, 2014). The two classes of public officials are strictly controlled by various government rules and represent a classic bureaucratic mechanism of public administration with a hierarchy at all levels of government. In this regard, the top-down machine of political and administrative decision making has become extremely strong and unambiguous, leaving almost no room for discretion or administrative autonomy at the lower levels of power.

One of the main challenges in the continuous attempts to transform public administration has been the efforts aimed at changing the behavioral aspects in the system – i.e. changing the traditional mindset of public servants working in the sphere to prepare them for new administrative functions where the reformation of the national economy after the collapse of the old command system became a number one priority. In this regard, the paradox of the reforms is that they have been carried out by those who had been educated by the old school of public administration since almost all important political posts have been occupied during the first years of independence by the former members of the Communist Party and graduates of the old political academy. For example, after the collapse of communism, many countries of in Eastern Europe fundamentally changed the structure of the old public administration system (Welsh, 1996), in most cases, simply by appointing new people to the posts. In Kazakhstan and many other post-Soviet nations, especially in Central Asia, the structure of the old bureaucratic systems had remained intact for many years after the moment they gained independence. Almost all structures of the central and local government have continued to use the same methods of public administration and governance as before, whether it was related to the work of government agencies, police, educational or healthcare institutions. Therefore, the public servant's mindset has been one of the fundamental challenges to change in the reforms. In this regard, the e-government projects are facing the same fundamental impediment, especially when it comes to promoting projects such as open data-driven e-participation and peer-to-peer platforms that require some degree of collaboration and down-top cooperation, which has never been practiced before. In this respect, the traditional bureaucratic machine is much more effective when the political leadership requires the fulfillment of direct commands and issues clear top-down instructions on what is allowed.

Key features of public administration

1 The public administration system of Kazakhstan is still under the process of reformation
2 The administrative structure of government at all levels has a strict top-down system of decision-making with no room for discretion
3 The traditions of the old bureaucratic mechanism and mentality are still strong

Implications for e-government

CHALLENGES

One of the key challenges in the implementation of the e-government projects, especially of those that require some degree of discretion, is that often public servants and administrators of e-government regard the program's creation as part of the numerous administrative reforms that they have to fulfill. The notorious formality often accompanies the realization of the projects where only direct administrative commands or political scrutiny become signals for activity in this direction. In this regard, such new aspects of the e-government development as collaboration with the third parties and public is misunderstood or ignored as unnecessary or too risky for the political status quo.

PROMISES

The promise of the new trends in reforming public administration in Kazakhstan, such as the division of the structure into two separate classes of public servants – political and administrative ones – and overall slowly increasing understanding of the importance of operating with e-government as an additional instrument in measuring general qualifications of civil servants, could potentially provide new incentives for government agents to pay special attention to the realization of the projects in the sphere. In addition, political public servants who represent the small but influential layer of policy makers are beginning to see some political motivation to improve the work of the e-government systems under their control since the overall realization of the project is considered the most important part of public sector reforms.

The economy of Kazakhstan: perils of the lopsided economy

Kazakhstan can be described as a country whose economic prosperity at the moment depends on global prices for natural resources due to a high dependency on the extractive industry and the overall large share of the sector in the national economy. Despite efforts of the central government to wean the economy from the mineral industry – for example the launch of projects to promote the industrial revolution in Kazakhstan and facilitate the development of the ICT-driven clusters at the regions – its role in the national market is still important, if not crucial, making the national economy vulnerable to external economic factors such as rapid changes in oil prices (Kutan & Wyzan, 2005). Indeed, the aftereffects of recent fluctuations in the global commodity markets are clearly indicative of the unsustainable nature of the lopsided economy that overly relies on revenues from the export of natural resources. The recent downfall of prices for oil, gas and other raw materials such as ferrous and nonferrous metals, which the country is also rich with, has led to significant budget cuts and partly even rapid devaluation of the national currency – Kazakh tenge (KZT) – in February 2014 and August 2015.

In this respect, one of the challenges of the economic instability could be potential austerity measures in many spheres, including in the e-government. It is not a secret that many public ICT-driven projects in Kazakhstan are initiated and launched by the central government and the role of the budget money in a successful stance of the country in terms of e-government development, which progress has been reflected in various global e-government ratings recently, is crucial. Without public investments in the sphere, many projects will cease to exist.

On the other hand, the development of new e-government projects, especially those that promote cost-effective strategies of public spending and civic engagement, such as electronic public procurement and open data projects, might be regarded as additional ICT-driven public administration measures to battle corruption and advance knowledge of the economy with less public spending and a higher role of civil society and local communities in the development of various sectors of the economy, making the sphere more sustainable and self-reliant.

Another aspect of the economic development that affects the promotion of e-government, especially in a technological sense, is the fact that Kazakhstan is geographically situated far away from the major transportation and trade routes that connect the world, which leads to a higher cost of for infrastructural projects (Raballand, 2003) and hinders the import of information and communication technologies, making many e-government projects extremely expensive and non-rentable in the conditions of the market economy.

Key features

1   Lopsided raw material economy
2   High dependency on global prices for minerals
3   Austerity measures and budget cuts

Implications for e-government

CHALLENGES

The recent development of e-government projects in Kazakhstan has been possible due to generous direct spending and assignations from the national budget. In this regard, possible budget cuts in the economy caused by a significant decrease in revenues coming from the export of various natural resources might lead to the closure of many projects in the sphere.

PROMISES

The possible cuts in public spending in the e-government sphere could paradoxically promote less government-focused and more cost-effective projects, such as civic engagement and collaborative wiki or open data-driven initiatives, that usually require less money from the budget funds.

The telecommunication industry: it is all about infrastructure

The development of the information and communication technologies sphere in Kazakhstan is experiencing almost the same level of change as in any part of the developed world because the government pays special attention to the economy sector, recognizing the importance of the ICT-driven economy and the necessity for the promotion of high computer literacy among the population, especially among schoolchildren (Bhuiyan, 2010). For example, according the Kazakh Agency of Statistics, about two thirds of citizens have access to the Internet, while the level of computer literacy among adults reaches 71 percent (The Kazakh Agency of Statistics, 2015), making the country a regional leader in Central Asia in terms of the human factor readiness in the ICT sphere. One of the aspects of the ICT development in Kazakhstan is the popularity of mobile technologies and wireless broadband access to the Internet, such as the 3G and 4G connections. Free Wi-Fi zones in many public places such as cafes, libraries, universities, public buildings, airports, train stations, buses, etc., allow people to be connected and stay online almost twenty-four hours a day. These facts create a favorable environment for the successful promotion of e-government projects that usually by default require some computer literacy and widespread access to the ICT and Internet among the citizenry and are conducive for the development of an information society, potentially providing excellent opportunities for fundamental transformations in the economic, social and even political spheres.

One of the challenges in the overall development of ICT-related projects in Kazakhstan is the problem of the so-called digital divide (Bhuiyan, 2010; Janenova, 2010) existing between various social and age groups of citizens and the difference in the development of the local telecommunication infrastructure that could be found between various regions of the country. In general, as in any part of the world, there is an overall trend that the young citizens and those who live in urban areas have higher computer literacy than the older generation and people residing in the countryside. In addition, some regions are experiencing significant problems with building the modern ICT infrastructure since there is a lack of economic incentives for telecommunication companies to invest in the regions due to the small population and remoteness of the areas. As a result, the development of the e-government projects in some regions of the country are challenged because there is low e-participation from the local communities, which could experience problems with even basic access to the Internet.

Key features of the telecommunication industry

1   General high level of computer literacy
2   High penetration of the Internet
3   Digital divide between citizens and regions

Implications for e-government

CHALLENGES

The problems of the digital divide such as those that exist between younger and older generations or between urban areas and the countryside create challenges for the development of various e-government projects that focus on e-participation and civic engagement.

The efforts of the central and local governments to promote special courses aimed at battling the computer illiteracy among the older generation, the overall policy to promote widespread access to the ICT due to low custom duties for imported telecommunication equipment and goods, and the simple fact that Kazakhstan has recently entered at last the WTO, which greatly simplifies the import of know-how create a favorable environment for the development of the e-government-related initiatives.

The nongovernmental sector: engaging the civil society

The development of the nongovernmental sector in Kazakhstan is probably one of the most controversial aspects in various political debates about the country's progress toward democracy and the topic is regarded as a sensitive one. For many years, the government has closely regulated the development of the NGOs in an attempt to negate foreign influence and funding. Moreover, the plans to promote indirect state financing through instruments such as grants and public procurement in the nongovernmental sector may result in a high dependency of the sphere on support from the national budget (The United Nations Radio, 2015).

Although there are many NGOs that do important work in helping the state to improve the lives of the local population in many aspects of social development (Diachenko, 2008), especially through consulting and charity activities, many of the registered organizations do not exist *de facto* or their activity is not relevant to the needs of the society in Kazakhstan (Luong & Weinthal, 1999).

In this respect, the development of the ICT sphere, especially of the open data concept, provides new opportunities for international, national and local NGOs to participate in the creation of various open data-driven initiatives aimed at advancing e-participation and civic engagement components of the e-government. Projects that would focus on helping local communities to battle corruption and poverty, mapping better transportation routes and crime areas, regulating lobbying activity and tracking safety standards in the commercial sector, etc., could potentially transform the traditional mechanism of e-government promotion, increasing the role of civil society and civic engagement, which, in turn, could facilitate the development of political culture and a new public mindset, letting behind the black box algorithm of the e-government building where the role of the public agencies was crucial – i.e. making it more user-driven and presumably more sustainable.

Key features of the nongovernmental sector

1   Overall development of the nongovernmental sphere controlled by government
2   Weak civil society and political culture due to the totalitarian past
3   High activity of NGOs in nonpolitical spheres

Implications for e-government

CHALLENGES

One of the challenges one can anticipate in the development of the NGOs in the e-government sphere is a high level of government regulation and control over the activity of the sector in the political and social life of the country, especially in terms of foreign financing. Many organizations that promote e-government in the world are administered and funded by various global development and charity funds. In this regard, they may face huge administrative and bureaucratic challenges in registering officially in Kazakhstan.

PROMISES

The new trends in the development of e-government in the sphere, such as the increasing popularity of the open data-driven, e-participation and wiki projects, where the importance of government is gradually decreasing and minimized to only the role of information and data provider, create promising opportunities for the nongovernmental sector to be more proactive in launching third-party platforms and applications aimed at facilitating the development of civil society and civic engagement.

The mass media sphere: harnessing the potential of PR

The media sphere is one of the most dynamically developing sectors of the local economy. The diversity of print and electronic mass media outlets, represented by national and international players in the area, allows citizens to be aware of domestic and global news and events. One of the notorious features of the local media market is strong regulation by government (Kenny & Gross, 2008) and high dependency of many media outlets on funding from the state budget through various grants and public procurement. Therefore, both national and local mass media, as well as government-owned and sometimes even commercial media structures, have to fulfill the contracts on propagating the government work in various spheres (Terry, 2005), including the e-government area. Mostly these channels of political communication play a double role, first, as an effective and useful instrument to inform the public about the e-government projects and, second, as an additional tool of the domestic political PR aimed at improving the image of the central government and political leadership among constituents.

Taking into account that many media programs, especially in television and newspapers, are realized in accordance with the public procurement contracts in the sphere; public teaching and PR campaigns in the e-government area are provided on a regular and systematic basis, dramatically increasing public coverage of the project and overall propagating effect on audiences. The public media coverage of the e-government projects is regarded as part of the general policy to educate citizens on the basics of computer literacy and, therefore, such TV programs and shows are transmitted at the national and local levels both in Kazakh and Russian languages. Some of the programs are shown even in English on the Kazakh TV channel (The Kazakh TV channel, 2015). In addition, some regions of the nearby Russian Federation and China are covered by the TV signal from Kazakhstan, which helps to provide information to the widespread Kazakh diasporas in both countries. Moreover, such international media outlets as CNN, BBC and Euronews are used as an additional tool of the country's image making on a commercial basis, including in the ICT sphere, demonstrating on these television channels and websites the attractive image of the nation for international audience to catch the attention of foreign investors and tourists.

This *sui generis* global public relations policy in the sphere has both positive and negative effects on the development of e-government in Kazakhstan. On the one hand, the fact that the implementation of the e-government policy is regarded as a matter of national priority means that everything that is even indirectly connected with the sphere will catch the attention of central government authorities. On the other hand, the overplay with the relentless attempts to improve the e-government image of the country in various international ratings and expensive PR campaigns and strategies not only demands significant financial resources but often means that the policy makers and developers have to pay special attention to the aspects of the e-government development that are the most results-oriented in terms of boosting the ranking rather than improving the operation of e-government, ignoring the development of areas that require fundamental changes in public mindset and political efforts rather than just investments in technologies, such as promotion of civic engagement and e-participation.

Key features of the mass media sphere

1 Diversity of the media market in Kazakhstan
2 Overall development of the media sphere strictly controlled by government
3 Many national and commercial media outlets directly or indirectly funded by government

Implications for e-government

CHALLENGES

Probably, one of the key challenges with the development of e-government is that the e-government policy itself is regarded more as a domestic and even global tool of political PR rather than an instrument of public administration. Therefore, many efforts of the government in the sphere are aimed at improving the e-government image of the country in various ratings and any achievements in the sphere are often used in mass media as a reference of the successful political and administrative reforms in various political debates and discourse.

PROMISES

The key promise of the ICT-driven public sector reforms in Kazakhstan is a political motivation of the central government to improve some aspects of the e-government development, especially if they require only administrative help, technological support or direct funding could easily lead to measurable results and achievements. Therefore, many e-government projects in the public administration system have great potential to be successfully realized and implemented. In this regard, the readiness of the central government to support any media projects aimed at boosting public knowledge about e-government helps to improve the overall development of the concept and raise public awareness.

The foreign policy: national interests or global branding?

It may seem that the foreign policy and international relations of the country have no connection to the e-government topic. However, in case of Kazakhstan, this factor of the e-government policy plays a crucial role in the overall development of the concept. The realization of the project is regarded by the national authorities as a matter of global image promotion, which the government authorities regard as one of the most important aspects of foreign policy and country image building in the international arena (Marat, 2009) in a manner described by Cummings (2003) as "pragmatic." Since any achievements in the area are documented today by global e-government experts, particularly, from the United Nations and World Bank, and reflected in the annual or biennial rating lists related to the sphere, this direction of foreign policy is beginning to play an increasingly important role, too. Therefore, the central government pays special attention to the global PR in the sphere and, in general, this aspect of the e-government development might be regarded as one of the important external factors of the concept's promotion in Kazakhstan. For many years, these ratings have played an important role as a political incentive for the government to initiate and improve its stance in global e-government ratings. The realization of the concept, along with ambitious projects such as the World Expo 2017 and the chairmanship of the country in the Organization for Security and Coopera-tion in Europe in 2010 (Melvin, 2009) were all regarded as part of the global PR campaign of the government. In this regard, the principle of persuasion plays its role not only in domestic politics (Schatz, 2008) but also as an important instrument of propaganda in the international arena.

One of the implications of the international policy is that the govern-ment agencies that realize the various e-government projects in Kazakhstan often invite foreign experts and policy entrepreneurs from other countries with a double goal: on the one hand, to get acquainted with new knowl-edge and best methods and practices in e-government building, and on the other hand, to share and make new professional connections with global e-government policy makers. The combination of this PR strategy and for-eign policy apparently proved to be effective. It was one of the reasons why Kazakhstan was honored to organize the Third Global e-Government Forum in September 2014 in the capital city of Astana, whose preparations offered a great motivation for the nation to promote the development of var-ious projects in the e-government area. The preparations to the World Expo that being organized in Kazakhstan for 2017 provide additional incentives for the decision makers in the sphere to focus on technological advance-ment in this direction, too.

Key features of foreign policy

1 The improvement of the global image of the country has been a crucial part of its foreign policy since the first years of independence
2 The national government pays special attention to the global ranking of the country in various e-government rating lists
3 Any achievements of the country in the international arena are used by the central government as an additional tool of persuasion in domestic politics

Implications for e-government

CHALLENGES

When developing various e-government projects, the policy makers try to pay more attention to the spheres that could potentially guarantee quick results and obvious achievements rather than to those that require greater efforts and time, but which are nevertheless important for further progress in this direction, especially taking into account the fact that many traditional strategies and tactics of e-government building are not as effective as before and the experts from the international organizations who compile the global ratings began to pay special attention to the policies that require more attention to the realization of such co-factors in building e-government as e-participation and collaboration with civil society.

PROMISES

The promotion of the e-government policy is regarded as one of the priorities in the technological development of the country, the results of which the national authorities plan to exhibit during the World Expo in 2017, this direction of the public sector reforms will be part of the agenda both in domestic and foreign policy of the central government, providing opportunities for the development of new projects in the sphere.

References

Abdrazak, P. K., & Musa, K. S. (2015). The impact of the cosmodrome "Baikonur" on the environment and human health. *International Journal of Biology and Chemistry*, *9*(1), 26–29.

Bader, M. (2011). Hegemonic political parties in post-Soviet Eurasia: Towards party-based authoritarianism? *Communist and Post-Communist Studies*, *44*(3), 189–197.

Bhuiyan, S. H. (2010). E-government in Kazakhstan: Challenges and its role to development. *Public Organization Review*, *10*(1), 31–47.

Bowyer, A. C. (2008). *Parliament and political parties in Kazakhstan*. Washington, D.C.: Central Asia-Caucasus Institute & Silk Road Studies Program, Johns Hopkins University-SAIS.

Brown, B. (1990). The public role in perestroika in central Asia. *Central Asian Survey*, *9*(1), 87–96.

Carlsen, L., Kenessov, B. N., Batyrbekova, S. Y., & Nauryzbaev, M. K. (2010). On the space activities at the Baikonur cosmodrome: An approach to an integrated environmental assessment. *International Journal of Environmental Sciences*, *1*, 55–64.

The Center of Government Efficiency Evaluation (2014). http://www.bagalau.kz/ru/med/smi/i224

Cummings, S. N. (2003). Eurasian bridge or murky waters between east and west? Ideas, identity and output in Kazakhstan's foreign policy. *Journal of Communist Studies and Transition Politics*, *19*(3), 139–155.

Diachenko, S. (2008). *The government and NGOs in Kazakhstan: Strategy, forms, and mechanisms of cooperation*. Sweden: CA&CC Press.

Diener, A. C. (2002). National territory and the reconstruction of history in Kazakhstan. *Eurasian Geography and Economics*, *43*(8), 632–650.

The E-Culture Project (2015). http://www.madenimura.kz/en/

The E-Government of Kazakhstan (2015). www.egov.kz

The E-History Project (2015). http://e-history.kz/en

Emrich-Bakenova, S. (2009). Trajectory of civil service development in Kazakhstan: Nexus of politics and administration. *Governance*, *22*(4), 717–745.

Isaacs, R. (2011). *Party system formation in Kazakhstan: Between formal and informal politics* (Vol. 26). London and New York: Routledge.

Janenova, S. (2010). E-Government in Kazakhstan: Challenges for a transitional country. In *18th NISPAcee Annual Conference "Public Administration in Times of Crisis"* (pp. 12–14). Warsaw, Poland.

Kassen, M. (2015). *Understanding systems of e-Government: E-Federalism and e-Centralism in the United States and Kazakhstan*. Lanham, MD: Lexington Books.

The Kazakh Agency of Statistics (2015). http://www.stat.gov.kz

The Kazakh TV Channel (2015). http://kazakh-tv.kz

Kendirbaeva, G. (1997). Migrations in Kazakhstan: Past and present. *Nationalities Papers, 25*(4), 741–751.

Kenny, T., & Gross, P. (2008). Journalism in Central Asia: A victim of politics, economics, and widespread self-censorship. *The International Journal of Press/Politics, 13*(4), 515–525.

Kutan, A. M., & Wyzan, M. L. (2005). Explaining the real exchange rate in Kazakhstan, 1996–2003: Is Kazakhstan vulnerable to the Dutch disease?. *Economic Systems, 29*(2), 242–255.

Luong, P. J., & Weinthal, E. (1999). The NGO paradox: Democratic goals and non-democratic outcomes in Kazakhstan. *Europe-Asia Studies, 51*(7), 1267–1284.

Marat, E. (2009). Nation branding in Central Asia: A new campaign to present ideas about the state and the nation. *Europe-Asia Studies, 61*(7), 1123–1136.

Melvin, N. J. (2009). The European Union, Kazakhstan and the 2010 OSCE Chairmanship. *Security and Human Rights, 20*(1), 42–47.

Micklin, P. (2007). The Aral sea disaster. *Annual Review of Earth and Planetary Sciences, 35*, 47–72.

Ohayon, I. (2013). The Kazakh famine: The beginnings of sedentarization. *Mass Violence & Resistance: An Interdisciplinary Online Journal*. Paris: The Paris Institute of Political Studies. http://www.sciencespo.fr/mass-violence-war-massacre-resistance/en/document/kazakh-famine-beginnings-sedentarization

Olcott, M. B. (1981). The collectivization drive in Kazakhstan. *Russian Review, 40*(2), 122–142.

Perlman, B. J., & Gleason, G. (2007). Cultural determinism versus administrative logic: Asian values and administrative reform in Kazakhstan and Uzbekistan. *International Journal of Public Administration, 30*(12–14), 1327–1342.

Pianciola, N. (2001). The collectivization famine in Kazakhstan, 1931–1933. *Harvard Ukrainian Studies, 25*(3/4), 237–251.

Polian, P. M. (2004). *Against their will: The history and geography of forced migrations in the USSR*. Budapest and New York: Central European University Press.

Raballand, G. (2003). Determinants of the negative impact of being landlocked on trade: An empirical investigation through the Central Asian case. *Comparative Economic Studies, 45*(4), 520–536.

Schatz, E. (2008). Transnational image making and soft authoritarian Kazakhstan. *Slavic Review, 67*(1), 50–62.

Simon, S. L., Baverstock, K. F., & Lindholm, C. (2003). A summary of evidence on radiation exposures received near to the Semipalatinsk nuclear weapons test site in Kazakhstan. *Health Physics, 84*(6), 718–725.

Stier, S. (2015). Political determinants of e-government performance revisited: Comparing democracies and autocracies. *Government Information Quarterly, 32*(3), 270–278.

Takada, J., Hoshi, M., Nagatomo, T., Yamamoto, M., Endo, S., Takatsuji, T., . . . Tchaijunusova, N. J. (1999). External doses of residents near Semipalatinsk nuclear test site. *Journal of Radiation Research, 40*(4), 337–344.

Terry, V. (2005). Postcard from the Steppes: A snapshot of public relations and culture in Kazakhstan. *Public Relations Review, 31*(1), 31–36.

The United Nations Radio (2015). http://www.unmultimedia.org/radio/russian/archives/203611/

Warf, B. (2013). The Central Asian digital divide. In M. Ragnedda & G. Muschert (Eds.), *The digital divide: The Internet and social inequality in international perspective* (pp. 270–281). London and New York: Routledge.

Welsh, H. A. (1996). Dealing with the communist past: Central and East European experiences after 1990. *Europe-Asia Studies, 48*(3), 413–428.

The Zhilstroysberbank Project (2015). www.hcsbk.kz

3 A retrospective analysis of e-government development in Kazakhstan

The development of e-government in Kazakhstan can be regarded as an example of the ICT-driven reforms in public administration in a typical emerging nation. Hypothetically, one of the primary reasons for the policy is a relentless desire of the central authorities to increase the global ranking of the country in various e-government listings and ratings. In fact, since the introduction of the state-run e-government program in 2004, which implementation was eventually materialized in the inauguration of the official e-government portal in 2006, the policy makers of the project have regarded the realization of the concept as a matter of national priority. Therefore, large-scale financial and human resources have been utilized to introduce and maintain technological, social and political components of the project. In this regard, the main purpose of this chapter is to analyze the development of the ICT-driven public sector reforms in Kazakhstan, where e-government has played a crucial role in the overall reformation of the technological and philosophical aspects of modern public administration and governance.

The framework for retrospective analysis

Introduction: identifying the milestones

In researching the history of the e-government project in Kazakhstan, it is necessary to section it to several periods in its development that would reflect the milestones of the ICT-driven reforms both in public administration – i.e. in the traditional domain of the concept – and in the political sphere, which surprisingly is beginning to indirectly affect the realization of many initiatives in the e-government area today. Moreover, the development of the concept is not only limited to the public sector, areas as economy and civil society were affected by the phenomenon, too, especially when it comes to, for example, the promotion of public procurement or e-commerce platforms and the recent emergence of new instruments such as open data and blog platforms to diffuse civic engagement and e-participation respectively, not only at the central national level of government but also at the regions and municipalities levels. These changes in the public sector could potentially affect in a positive way even the traditional behavioral aspects of e-government communication by welcoming new players to collaborate in some of the ICT-driven public projects – i.e. resorting to a practice that has never been used before in the political life of the country. It could be especially beneficial in a country that is still experiencing the consequences of its totalitarian Soviet past. The cumbersome and extremely bureaucratic public administration system that it inherited as a legacy from the USSR in 1991 is a notorious example to mention in this respect.

Methodology: asking the research questions

The research will be based mostly on a retrospective analysis of the e-government policies realized by Kazakhstan during the last decade – i.e. since 2004, when the first national e-government strategy was adopted – and will mainly rely on the study of the secondary sources and data on the topic such as academic and professional literature, policy analysis of the main political strategies adopted in this period, content analysis of the text of related legislation, political programs and speeches by top public figures and key policy makers in the sphere. In this regard, the retrospective analysis of the e-government development will be built around the following research questions (see figure 3.1):

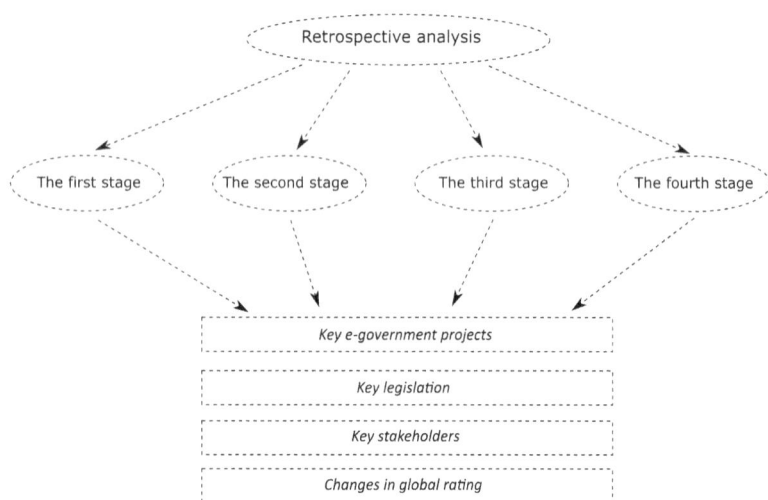

Figure 3.1 Building the framework of the retrospective analysis

Source: own illustration

1   What were the key e-government projects?
2   How was the e-government sphere regulated?
3   Who were the key e-government stakeholders?
4   How did the development of the projects affect the global e-government rating of Kazakhstan over time?

The history of e-government in Kazakhstan: coming of age

The first period (2004–2006): building the e-government infrastructure

Key projects

THE OFFICIAL E-GOVERNMENT PORTAL

The main characteristic of the first period is the preparation to launch the first e-government project, which was finalized with the inauguration of the official portal in 2006. Officially, the start of the preparations began in 2004 with the introduction of the first e-government strategy (The e-Government Directive # 1471, 2004), adopted by the central government as a main political document for all ICT-based transformations in government and public administration. Conceptually, the strategy was developed under the strong influence of international trends at that time after nearly all developed and many developing nations had adopted similar e-government programs (Moon, 2002; Chadwick & May, 2003; Lee, Tan & Trimi, 2005). Therefore, one of the primary goals of the concept was to offer a road map for general political promotion of the ICT-based public administration and develop concrete tactics on how to better implement a single e-government project with some potentially beneficial areas to focus on such as the development of technological components, which would include the portal itself and a set of initial electronic services (e-services). In this regard, it is necessary to note that these plans did not propose any e-services in the modern sense (Venkatesh, Chan & Thong, 2012). Mainly, e-services were understood as a set of ordinary government information, but the organization on a single portal, however, was better focused on particular areas of government activity. Basically, it offered information aggregated from various government websites. The portal itself (www.e.gov.kz) was introduced to the public on April 12, 2006, which from the first day of operation has provided free access to several information services (Kassen, 2010) in sections such as culture and leisure, environment protection, land management, transport, travel and others.

For the overall realization of the e-government project in 2005–2007, including the launch and operation of the portal, the central government allocated approximately 52 billion KZT (The e-Government Directive # 1471, 2004), which was equivalent to 400 million USD at that time. Money was spent on the infrastructural and organizational preparations for the launch of the official e-government project. In this regard, one of the organizational parts of the ICT-driven public sector reforms was the unification of all identification numbers such taxpayer, passport and ID, and social security numbers of citizens into one single national identification number to ensure better integration of various e-government systems and databases and, more important, provide a single technological venue for the launch of transactional services in the future. Kazakhstan, in this respect, just followed the widespread global trend (Otjacques, Hitzelberger & Feltz, 2007; McKenzie, Crompton & Wallis, 2008; Lyon, 2009) in this direction of ICT-driven public administration reforms.

MANAGEMENT OF INTERNET DOMAINS

Another aspect of the ICT-driven public sector reforms in Kazakhstan was the first attempts to regulate the national segment of the Internet space by differentiating special domain names for various sectors of the economy in a Western manner, which would include names such as edu.kz for educational institutions (e.g. universities, academies and colleges); gov.kz for government agencies; org.kz for nongovernmental organizations and civic projects; net.kz for telecommunication companies, etc. (The decree N 88-b, 2005). However, the plans in this area have not been fully realized, since not all government agencies followed the rules in registering their official websites and portals. The financial and organizational complexity to re-register thousands of domain names, especially in the private sector, would require public support and presented a bureaucratic and technological challenge for many organizations and small businesses. The registration of many more websites in the following years occurred in an environment of political and legal uncertainty of what should be done with existing and newly registered websites and how to regulate the domain registration, which just reinforced the status quo in this sector of the ICT market and the project was abandoned.

Regulation policy

ADOPTION OF THE FIRST E-GOVERNMENT STRATEGY

The strategy of e-government realization, adopted in 2004 and officially named the state program of e-government formation in the Republic of Kazakhstan for 2005–2007 became a key legal instrument to regulate all public activities in this direction for the following three years. In addition to the provision of various information and prospective transactional services, the administrators of the program planned to implement several measures aimed at closing the digital divide (The e-Government Directive # 1471, 2004), which was one of the main barriers of e-government adoption in Kazakhstan at that time among citizens (Bhuiyan, 2010) and between regions, for example, by organizing special courses and educational programs. Another goal was to ensure some degree of information security of the governmental infrastructure related to the implementation of the e-government project, by protecting databases and telecommunication networks from external tampering activity.

AMENDMENTS TO THE RELATED E-GOVERNMENT LAWS

At that time, the development of the telecommunication market was virtually monopolized by Kazakhtelecom (McGlinchey & Johnson, 2007), a national telecommunication carrier, which controlled the ICT networks of the entire country and provided access to the Internet not only to the vast majority of subscribers among citizens and businesses but also to other Internet service providers. Taking into account the fact that the development of e-government logically implied the organization of affordable and easy access to the Internet for a greater number of citizens, especially in the country, the national government decided to ensure the creation of specialized access points to the Web in all schools, resorting to a wide telecommunication and infrastructural basis of the carrier (Resolution N 479, 2005). Another goal was to cut prices for access to the Internet for all citizens of the country to ensure the formation of an army of potential users for the normal operation of future e-government projects. In this respect, the national authorities resorted to traditional bureaucratic top-down mechanisms of regulation such as resolutions and directives, which nevertheless, as it later turned out, have proved to be effective in a highly monopolized telecommunications market.

Key stakeholders of the projects

GOVERNMENT AGENCIES

The national government was a key stakeholder in promoting the e-government project, whose support and readiness to fund the related activities in this direction allowed political funding for the realization of the e-government strategy. The strategy was developed by the Agency of Informatization and Communication, which also provided administrative supervision and strategic direction associated with launching the e-government portal. Therefore, the agency de facto might be regarded as an official administrator of the e-government project in Kazakhstan, representing and acting on behalf of the national government at that time, since it follows direct instructions coming from the Presidential Administration, the Office of the Prime Minister and other central agencies. Ministries and agencies such as the Ministry of Economy, Committee of National Security and Ministry of Justice also play certain roles in advancing the project, providing some administrative support and assistance in the corresponding areas.

NATIONAL COMPANIES

The lion's share of the technical assistance and maintenance for the e-government project was provided by state-owned telecommunication companies, especially, JSC National Information Technologies. In fact, all technological development of the related e-government systems and databases was provided by ICT specialists from the company under the political and administrative control of central government agencies. In this regard, the case of Kazakhstan provides a classic example of the e-government realization strategy implemented in a typical unitary state where the role of the national authorities in the development of various projects, including in the e-government sphere, is crucial, since the participation of the regional authorities is minimal because they are all subjects of direct control from the central government with little or no room for discretion in making any significant political or even administrative decisions. In this respect, the realization of the e-government program was carried out at the central level both politically and technologically by the national government. The obvious result of the policy was the creation of a single e-government portal with single databases and single e-services for the entire country without subdivision for regional and local projects. The participation of the representatives from the nongovernmental sector such as the NGOs, research centers, and universities was virtually nonexistent.

The international perspective

It is necessary to note that Kazakhstan had been the subject of international scrutiny in the sphere even before the e-government project was officially inaugurated in 2006, especially in various rating lists compiled by the United Nations, the World Economic Forum, Waseda University and *The Economist* magazine about the development of the ICT-driven public sector reforms in the country, especially in the regional context. For example, in 2003, according to the Global e-Government Index provided by the United

Nations Public Administration Network (UNPAN, 2003), Kazakhstan was regarded as a country with a fairly weak presence of government agencies on the Internet and, therefore, the country occupied only a mediocre 83rd place in the ratings, behind nations such as Belarus and Tongo. However, in the next annual ratings in 2004 and 2005, Kazakhstan reached the 69th and 65th places, respectively (UNPAN, 2004; UNPAN, 2005), demonstrating a dramatic change in the ranking, which was explained by the strategic initiatives and efforts of the nation to integrate various ICT-driven public administration systems and tools into one single project with the main focus on providing organized information services (see table 3.1).

Another reason of the upgrade in the ranking was an outreach-oriented approach used by the administrators of the e-government projects in providing almost all content not only in Kazakh and Russian, two working languages in Kazakhstan but, what was important, also in English even in the information sections of the websites and sets of e-services that were originally designed only for the use by local population, which is indicative that it was an additional and, as it later turned out, effective PR step to draw the attention of the international audience and, apparently, the experts from the UN, who assessed the websites, about the changes in the portals.

The second period (2007–2009): integrating e-government into a single platform

The second period of e-government development in Kazakhstan could be characterized as the period between 2007 and 2009 when all e-government projects were finally integrated into the single domain of the concept both in political and technological senses. Another feature of the period is clarification of the official stakeholders in various e-government programs and determination of the primary venues of administrative and technological support. This period is also associated with the first results of the e-government development in Kazakhstan and the benefits that its realization brought into the public domain such as a dramatic increase in the assortment of

Table 3.1 Changes in global e-government rankings of Kazakhstan from 2003 to 2005

	Global rating of the national e-government project		
	2003	*2004*	*2005*
Kazakhstan	83th	69th	65th

Source: elaboration based on data from UNPAN (2003, 2004, 2005)

e-services and emergence of new projects that helped to identify the best ways on how to battle such notorious aspects of public administration as red tape and corruption.

Key projects

E-PUBLIC PROCUREMENT PROJECT

One of the most effective e-government initiatives launched during that period was the e-procurement project aimed at providing greater regulation in the sphere of public procurement and public contracts of government agencies with the business sector through ICT. Officially, the project was initiated in 2007 as an experimental platform to test the possibilities of the new system of public procurement in government agencies (The public e-procurement project, 2015). One of the goals of the project was to create an effective system of budget planning and control over public procurement operations (Obi & Iwasaki, 2015) in all government agencies both at the central and local levels. In building the platform, organizers applied the same approach as with the realization of the e-government project, focusing on providing a single-entry venue for all activities in the sphere such as a single portal, single databases and choosing a single operator. Therefore, one of the important steps during that period of the e-procurement project was the creation of the registry of potential public contractors and government agencies. Another goal of the project was to save significant budget money by transferring all public contracts in the sphere into an electronic format and, indirectly, presumably decreasing possibilities of corruption in the sphere due to a higher level of transparency in the electronic operations and greater accountability of government agencies in the system.

ONLINE CONFERENCES PROJECT

Another new project aimed at promoting the e-government, especially in outreaching the concept via mass media, was the online conference project (The Online Conference Platform, 2015). The initiative was launched in 2007 as a special online platform that would help central government agencies establish better communication channels with the citizenry through instruments such as online conferences of the top government executives both at the central and local level on a regular basis. The portal of e-government, which was launched the year before, was regarded as the only place for conducting such events due to the unitary feature of the public administration system that required a single control and administration in the sphere at all levels of power. Taking into account the importance of the project, President Nursultan Nazarbayev decided to be the first speaker at the session of the online conference organized in the portal of e-government on June 7, 2007. Later on, this practice became unofficially mandatory for all top government executives, since the participation in the online conferences was regarded as one of the important indicators in assessing political civil servants.

Regulation policy

THE NEW E-GOVERNMENT STRATEGY

The new e-government strategy that was adopted in 2007 provided an out-line for the government activities in the sphere for the next period from 2008 to 2010 (The Government Resolution N 1155–1, 2007), paying special attention to the development of new aspects of the e-government building in Kazakhstan such as e-municipalities (*e-akimats* in Kazakh), e-personnel, e-management, and e-legislation projects, which realization later proved to be too technologically or organizationally challenging or expensive to implement in such a short period of time. The overall budget funding of the anticipated reforms in the e-government sphere was expected to be about 23 billion KZT (approximately 190 million USD). It is interesting to note that the amount of allocated money was significantly less than during the previous period, since the first program was primarily aimed at preparing the infrastructural basis of the e-government project.

THE E-PROCUREMENT LAW

In order to ensure the smother development of the e-procurement project, the government of Kazakhstan adopted a special law in the area which pre-pared the legal basis for the introduction of the system (The E-Procurement Law, 2007). Adopted on July 21, 2007, the law paid special attention to the regulation of the electronic methods of public procurement and related activity of government agencies in the sphere (OECD, 2007). The new amendments that come into force in 2009 reinforced the document with new directions and regulatory mechanisms of control and administration in the anti-monopoly area. The key goal of the legal instrument was to pave the way for the administrators of the project to implement a single strategy in the area and provide clear overview for both government bodies and the business sector on the main aspects of the transactions in the public pro-curement sphere. This document provided a primary source of reference for the development of various guidebooks and instructions on details of the procedures.

Key stakeholders

GOVERNMENT AGENCIES

Along with the Agency of Informatization and Communication as a main administrator of the e-government program in Kazakhstan, there were new stakeholders representing the government. The Committee of the Financial Control and Public Procurement in the Ministry of Finance began to play an important role as the focal point for all administrative regulations in the sphere of electronic procurement for government agencies (IBP USA, 2009). The importance of the e-procurement project was partly aimed at reducing government spending and battling corruption and significantly raised the role of the Ministry of Finance. In addition, now the Agency of Informatization and Communication was obliged to report twice a year before the central government (The Government Resolution N 1155–1, 2007) about the realization of the program and track any progress in the realization of all e-government-related projects such as the creation of the e-corporate management system and e-procurement.

NATIONAL COMPANIES

The importance of the ICT-driven public sector reforms in Kazakhstan, including the realization of the e-government project for the reputation of the country in the international arena, predetermined the creation of a special info-communication holding (Zerde, 2015), which was accountable before the national government for all informatization projects. The new holding began to administer ICT projects such as the creation of the International Information Technology University (IITU, 2015) in cooperation with Carnegie-Mellon University from the United States and the creation of the KazSatNet project (KazSatNet, 2015) to prepare specialists in the IT sphere, including the needs of e-government and promoting the development of the satellite telecommunication technologies, respectively. The implementation of the e-procurement project raised the necessity to designate a special operator of the program that would advance the online system of public procurement on a single portal. Such organization as the Electronic Commerce Center became a key stakeholder of the project (ECC, 2015), which provided all procedural and technological assistance to the Ministry of Finance in this regard.

The international perspective

Despite the further development of e-government as well as the emergence and promotion of some new projects such as e-procurement and the creation of the IT University in Kazakhstan in 2007–2009, the overall project was assessed by experts from the UN, who now began to track the advancement of national e-government programs in the world on a biennial basis, which was reflected in the overall ranking of the country in the global e-government rating list published in 2008. The main reason was the weak development of e-services and the fact that Kazakhstan did not launch any transactional services despite some commitments to do so, which were clearly stipulated in the 2004 e-government strategy (The e-Government Directive # 1471, 2004). Therefore, the country experienced a dramatic downfall in the global e-government rating after 2005. For example, if in 2005 Kazakhstan occupied 65th place, then in 2008 the country was downgraded to the 81st rank, being surpassed by many developing nations (see table 3.2) (UNPAN, 2005, 2008).

The third period (2010–2012): focusing on interactive e-government

The third period of e-government development in Kazakhstan can be characterized as a milestone in the conceptual realization of the digital government idea and total transformation of the implementation strategies which are now aimed more at promoting transactional services, improving the layout and ergonomics of the project and, more important, at facilitating the development of the participation tools and platforms in an attempt to improve the global stance of the country in the e-government ratings and focusing on the projects that are closely watched and scrutinized by e-government experts from the UN.

Key projects

TRANSACTIONAL E-SERVICES

Obviously, the lessons of the significant downfall of the country's ranking in the global e-government rating have been learned by the administrators of the project since they were now beginning to pay special attention to

Table 3.2 The dramatic downgrade in the international rating of Kazakhstan in terms of e-government development (2005–2008)

	Global rating of the e-government readiness		
	2005	*2008*	*Change points*
Kazakhstan	65th place	81st place	−16

Source: elaboration based on data from UNPAN (2005, 2008)

the launch of the services, especially of those that are aimed at promoting e-participation and interactive aspects of the digital platforms in the sphere. The overall number of transactional services has dramatically risen since 2010 by the inclusion of areas of communication with citizens and businesses such as the launch of online tax reporting, online payments for government duties and community utilities, healthcare, education, etc. In addition to the launch of the transactional services (Bhuiyan, 2011), the e-government projects began to provide video guides and instructions on how to use better the opportunities that the platforms offered (The E-Government of Kazakhstan, 2015).

OPEN LAWS PROJECT

One of the useful features of the e-government development in Kazakhstan during that period of time was the launch of the online legislation project (The Adilet Open Laws Project, 2015) that began to provide free-of-charge access to the regulatory database that included the full texts of documents such as laws, ordinances, charters, rules and other legal acts adopted by government agencies both at the national and local levels of power. The project was regarded as one of the measures to close the knowledge divide that existed in the country since access to almost all legal documents before that had been provided only on a fee basis. Now anyone could access the databases to be acquainted with the legislation. The overall administration of the project was carried out by the Republican Center of Legal Information under the control of the Ministry of Justice (RCLI, 2015). This measure was positively met, especially by lawyers, researchers and students.

NEW DIGITAL ID CARDS

Another new feature related to the promotion of the e-government project was the issue of new ID cards with a function that allows using them as a digital signature certificate. This measure, which had been long ago practiced in many developed countries (Lyon, 2005; Arora, 2008), was designed presumably to improve the information security of the electronic transactions in communicating with the government systems and help to promote the interactive component of the entire project, focusing on services that require authorization and access to the databases with personal details and commercial secrets. The issue of the new IDs and associated digital devices such as special card readers and mobile paying terminals that usually could allow carrying out mobile transactions with the portal (Hung, Chang & Kuo, 2013) significantly simplified the mechanism of interaction with the entire system of e-government at the national level.

Regulation policy

THE INDUSTRIAL AND INNOVATION STRATEGY OF KAZAKHSTAN

Since e-government was beginning to be considered an intrinsic part of the overall innovational economy that the country had been trying to build since the declaration of its independence, the traditional practice with pro- viding a regulatory basis for the promotion of the related projects through the e-government strategy was replaced now with a single strategic docu- ment that would focus on various aspects of the technological development of the country from the perspective of general planning, administration and control in the sphere. The new document, which was adopted in 2010, was named The Forced Industrial and Innovation Development of Kazakhstan in 2010–2014 (The Directive N 958, 2010) and included aspects of gov- ernment activity in building the new economy such as the development of technological infrastructure and transportation, promotion of public-private partnership, information and communication technologies (including the advancement of various e-government projects), mapping of industrializa- tion zones, etc.

THE ICT DEVELOPMENT PROGRAM

Another document that regulated the development of e-government pro- jects in Kazakhstan during that period of time was the regulatory act named The Program of the Information and Communication Technology Devel- opment in Kazakhstan for 2010–2014 (Resolution N 983, 2010). The main idea of the document was to plan the progress of the ICT sphere in terms of regulation in the sphere, especially in standardization and prioritization of perspective directions of the innovational development and promo- tion of the best international practices in the area. In relationship to the implementation of the e-government projects, this legal instrument pro- vided new opportunities to streamline the existing e-services and outline the perspectives for the development of platforms such as social media- driven projects and blog platforms that significantly improved the overall progress of the e-government projects in the direction of e-participation.

Key stakeholders

GOVERNMENT AGENCIES

The development of the transactional services, the main idea of which was to realize at the central level the need to build a single-entry platform for all e-government-related services and interactions of citizens with public agencies both at the national and local levels, implied the increasing importance of all government agencies. Another reason for the unification was a policy aimed at developing only single databases for all e-government purposes in all agencies regardless whether it was ministry or department. In this respect, such a new government agency as the Ministry of Industry and New Technologies, which was later renamed as the Ministry of Investments and Development (MIDK, 2015) and Ministry of Justice (MJK, 2015) began to play one of the most important roles in promoting innovation projects in the ICT sector, including the e-government-driven public sector reforms.

MUNICIPALITIES

The general trend toward the development of single e-government databases has significantly increased the role of local governments in promoting the project, too, since many services that were popular among citizens at that time appeared to be related to the local issues and topics such as the application to municipal housing, access to the land cadastre, issue of real property and address certificates. Because Kazakhstan is a unitary state, all these services should be provided at the national level from a single e-government portal, using single data sets and single identification numbers, aggregating all available data from various government sources in one venue. Taking into account the size of the country and the presence of fourteen regions and two administrative units (the capital city Astana and megalopolis Almaty), the role of the local authorities in these processes was now beginning to play a role, too.

NATIONAL COMPANIES

The adoption of the Industrial and Innovation Strategy in 2010 predetermined the ever-increasing role of various ICT companies in promoting e-government, as one of the most important parts of the whole informatization in the public administration sector. As usual, these state-owned companies were indirectly administered and controlled by the central government agencies. In this regard, new players such as the National Innovation Fund, later renamed as the National Agency of Technological Development (NATD, 2015), and the Center for Engineering and Transfer of Technologies (CETT, 2015) were created to provide additional scientific and technological support for the administrators of these projects. Another goal of the new stakeholders was to attract foreign counterparts and import new information and communication technologies and expertise, including in the e-government sphere.

The international perspective

E-GOVERNMENT RANKING

The international image of the country in terms of e-government development was significantly improved during that period of time due to the promotion of several initiatives such as the launch of transactional services, development and integration of single databases and continuous promotion of the e-procurement project. The progress could be easily tracked through the national e-government ranking in the global rating provided by the UN during that period of time. For example, in 2010 the country occupied the 46th place in the world (UNPAN, 2010), demonstrating a dramatic change in comparison with 2008 when the ranking was 81st (UNPAN, 2008). Moreover, in the next biennial report on the development of the global e-government projects in 2012, the country reached a 38th place (UNPAN, 2012) (see table 3.3).

E-PARTICIPATION RANKING

Another indicator of e-government development, which began to be evaluated by UN experts in the rating as one of the most important aspects in measuring the interactive components of the entire project, was the e-participation part of e-government progress. In this regard, Kazakhstan demonstrated dramatic transformations in this area, too. For example, if in 2010 the ranking of the country in terms of the promotion of e-participation platforms was 18th, in 2012 Kazakhstan controversially was graded high (Åström et al., 2012; Linde & Karlsson, 2013), reaching second place in the world along with Singapore (UNPAN, 2012), a universally recognized leader in the e-participation index, surpassing many traditional leaders in the sphere (see table 3.4).

One of the reasons for the rapid change in the global ranking, according to the international panel of e-government experts from the UN who conducted the survey in 2012, was the launch of the interactive and transactional

Table 3.3 The comparison of the global e-government ranking of Kazakhstan in 2010 and 2012

	Global rating of the e-government readiness	
	2010	*2012*
Kazakhstan	46th place	38th place

Source: elaboration based on data from UNPAN (2010, 2012)

Table 3.4 The global top winners of the e-participation index in 2012

Rank	Country
1st place	Netherlands
	Korea
2nd place	Kazakhstan
	Singapore
3rd place	United Kingdom
	United States

Source: elaboration based on data from UNPAN (2012)

components of the e-government project in Kazakhstan and development of the new participatory tools such as blogging platforms of officials and public figures and social media networks projects within the public administration system (UNPAN, 2012) that were presumably aimed at promoting the new channels of political communication with citizens and mass media.

The fourth period (2013–present): opening e-government?

The fourth period of e-government development is probably one of the most interesting periods in the history of the phenomenon in Kazakhstan. The emergence on the horizon of new platforms to further the concept such as open government and open data, which are now actively implemented in many countries all over the world, and, what is more important, the necessity to promote, in this regard, civic participation and engagement, arguably two crucial components for the successful realization of any modern e-government project, provides both new opportunities and challenges for the policy makers in the realization of the idea in Kazakhstan. Therefore, this period can be regarded as critical and decisive for the future development of the paradigm in this Central Asian nation.

Key projects

OPEN DATA PLATFORM

The popularity of the open government concept around the world during the last six years under the influence of the United States, where the concept was born under the leadership of the U.S. President Barack Obama (Lathrop & Ruma, 2010; Harrison et al., 2011; Kassen, 2013) and whose promotion in the development of national e-government projects is regarded as one of the most important aspects of progress by many international experts in the sphere, provided an incentive to implement the similar open government projects in Kazakhstan, too. Apparently, the evaluation of the advancement in that direction of e-government development in the future will become a number one indicator of the national success in achieving higher ranking in the global e-government rating conducted today by the UN in the sphere of public administration. In this regard, one of the most important aspects of the open government concept is the development of open data projects, namely, the official open data portals and the promotion of the open data-driven projects, which is the main goal of the concept since open data in its original sense is just a set of government data sets published in a machine-readable format (Janssen, Charalabidis & Zuiderwijk, 2012). However, what is important is the possibility of its re-use and the opportunities for the promotion of political communication that it's processing by third parties (i.e. citizens and independent ICT developers) could now offer.

In this respect, it is important to promote political collaboration and civic engagement in the sphere, which will help to open up the black box of the traditional top-down directives-driven realization policies in the e-government sphere (Kassen, 2013) that would arguably require the transformation of the public mindset, especially in transitional societies like Kazakhstan, and definitely the political will to promote such political changes. In this respect, the realization of the open data project, which was started in 2013, is mostly regarded as part of the public administration reforms (The Open Government Project, 2015) that the government has been trying to reform for the last two decades rather than an aspect of the political transformations in the country, where the topic is considered to be controversial. The focus on the reformation of the public sector and economy is regarded as a number one priority, while discussions on the topics in the sphere are deemed to be too early and even perilous for social stability and political security.

The realization of the open data project could be considered as an experimental platform that is closely monitored by administrators and is implemented by the traditional way where government agencies provide data sets on a systematic basis on a single national open data portal, which is based on the same platform as the system of digital government, and generally should be regarded as an intrinsic part of the e-government project. Therefore, the same rules of the implementation policy, such as the presence of a single administrator and operator, as well as central funding and political control in the sphere, are applied in promoting the open data project.

THE MOBILE E-GOVERNMENT

Another important steppingstone in building the multidimensional aspects of e-government in Kazakhstan is the so-called mobile government or m-government, whose realization all over the world demonstrated dramatic growth in one decade from SMS-driven to multimedia-based e-services

(Kushchu & Kuscu, 2003; Al-Khamayseh, Lawrence & Zmijewska, 2006; Kushchu, 2007; Shareef, Archer & Dwivedi, 2012; Amailef & Lu, 2013). The growing popularity of various mobile gadgets and devices such as smartphones, tablet computers and mobile operating systems and platforms of related applications and programs offer new dimensions for the promotion of related software industry that provides opportunities to build new information products in almost any sphere, including in e-government area. In this regard, the mobile government is considered a miniature version of the traditional desktop variant of the e-government project with the same or limited number of e-services, the same set of security measures and authorization. One of the interesting aspects of the project in Kazakhstan is that it also provides access to transactional services such as interactive and various payment platforms. Taking into account the recent popularity of mobile devices, the m-government provides various applications based on such widespread operating platforms as Android and Apple iOS, dramatically increasing the popularity of the project among citizens of the country.

Regulation policy

THE STRATEGY INFORMATION KAZAKHSTAN–2020

One of the most interesting documents aimed at regulating the development of the ICT-driven public sector reforms is a strategy named The Information Kazakhstan 2020, which was adopted in early 2013. The main idea of the strategic document was to facilitate the development of the country in terms of advancement toward the information society where the role of the e-government-driven institutions such as new public administration and digital interaction with citizens would play a crucial role in the informatization of the social relationship (The Directive N 464, 2013). The realization of the document was divided into two periods: one is from 2013 to 2017, and the second one from 2018 to 2020 (see figure 3.2).

One of the goals of the plan was to reduce bureaucratic barriers in developing e-government services such as shortening the time of rendering the e-services to five days or facilitating the development of various open data-based services. It is also interesting to note that for the first time, the government put in concrete strategic goals that are specifically aimed at achieving progress that should be reflected in the global e-government rating of the country such as to enter the list of the five most-developed countries in terms of e-participation promotion or be on the list of the thirty most-advanced countries in terms of overall development of e-government in the world, indicating the strategic significance of e-government as an important project of the global country PR and international prestige.

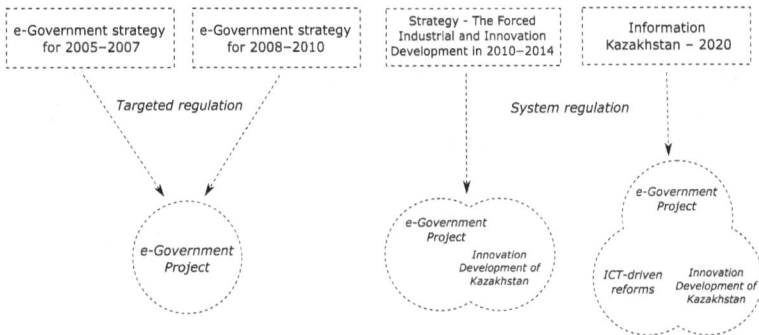

Figure 3.2 The evolution of e-government: from targeted to system regulation
Source: own illustration

THE STRATEGY FOR THE AGENCIES OF INFORMATIZATION
AND COMMUNICATION

The importance of the projects indicated in the strategy The Information Kazakhstan 2020 required fundamental changes in the work of the main administrator of almost all e-government projects – i.e. the Agency of Informatization and Communication, whose role as a public agency that represents the central government was crucial in many aspects. In this regard, the adoption of a special document in 2014 that would regulate the activity of the agency in terms of strategic development was one of the steps to cement the leading role of the organization in furthering projects in the sphere (Resolution N 369, 2014). One of the interesting aspects in promoting e-government was the organization of the data centers and special laboratories in areas such as cloud computing, big data, mobile and e-government technologies. Another goal of the agency was to facilitate the development of ICT-driven projects that would help to close the digital divide, especially in rural areas of the country.

Key stakeholders

GOVERNMENT AGENCIES

The growing importance of the ICT-driven public sector reforms and the necessity to focus on more collaborative aspects of e-government development in Kazakhstan required the fundamental transformation of the roles that the government agencies play in advancing the projects in the sphere at both national and local levels of power. It was related not only to the Agency of Informatization and Communication – i.e. the key stakeholder of almost all e-government platforms – but also to all ministries and local governments (*akimats*) and sometimes even national corporations that participate in some of the projects such as the informatization of the country in general, and the electronic public procurement portal or open data initiative, in particular, which is beginning to play an important role. The general rule is simple, the more popular e-services are in a particular area of e-government, the more important are the roles of the government agencies operating in the spheres. In this regard, agencies such as the Ministry of the National Economy (MNEK, 2015) and the Committee of Transport in the Ministry of Investments and Development (The Committee of Transport, 2015) are beginning to play an important role in the overall development of various e-government projects. Even the Parliament of Kazakhstan should be considered one of the key stakeholders in building e-government since the promotion of the open government concept is impossible without the realization of the open institutions in all branches of power.

KAZPOST AND KAZAKHTELECOM

The realization of the strategic document – The Information Kazakhstan 2020 – which includes many projects in the e-government sphere predetermined an important role of some of the national companies such as KazPost and Kazakhtelecom. KazPost is a national postal company (KazPost, 2015) that controls a lion's share of the domestic postal and parcel deliveries. One of the projects planned for the future is the initiative aimed at making the postal delivery process easier in terms of the interaction with the system and speedier through the development of modern electronic methods of tracking and delivery control. The system that was called the mobile postman is planned to be integrated with the mobile e-government platforms (Ospanova, 2015).

Kazakhtelecom is the largest telecommunications company in Kazakhstan (Kazakhtelecom, 2015), which controls a significant share of the market in spheres such as the provision of Internet services, being a monopolist in providing access to the landline broadband, fiber optic and 4G Internet in many regions of the country, cable television and satellite telecommunication services through its various subsidiaries, the largest of which are Astana Telecom and Almaty Telecom. In this regard, the most important role of the company in the area of the e-government promotion is the activity aimed at closing the digital divide by connecting the remote areas of the country to the modern telecommunication services either through its widespread network of service providers or using several telecommunication satellites recently launched into orbit for that purpose, and, finally, by cutting prices for the services.

The international perspective

The international perspective of the country in terms of e-government development was controversial in the global ratings in the sphere. On the one hand, the overall progress of the ICT-driven public sector reforms was easily noticed by the UN's e-government experts who usually evaluate the development of national projects in the area on a biennial basis. For example, if in 2012 the global e-government ranking of Kazakhstan was 38th place (UNPAN, 2012), by 2014 the position of the country has reached the 28th place (UNPAN, 2014), which is an obvious achievement at first glance. However, looking at the e-participation ranking of the country in the same biennial report published by the UN in 2014, one can easily notice the dramatic downgrade of the nation in the development of the participatory component of the e-government from a leading second position in the global list in 2012 to the mediocre 22th place in 2014 (UNPAN, 2014). One of the main reasons for the rapid downfall was a lack of progress in collaborative cooperation with the civil society and weak promotion of the open data projects in Kazakhstan, which is now beginning to play a crucial role in e-government ratings. The *carte blanche* that was given to the country in 2012 as a generous sign of confidence and support of promising commitments of the nation in terms of potential social and political transformations related to the e-government sphere, especially in civic engagement and peer-to-peer cooperation, has not been realized.

Summary of the retrospective analysis: key findings

In general, because of the active implementation of e-government strategy and the promotion of various related ICT-driven public sector reforms, the overall global rating of the e-government project during the last decade has demonstrated steady growth (see table 3.5).

However, further progress in this direction will require new approaches on how to address better the challenges of the implementation policies in building a collaborative e-government since recent trends in the development of the concept are experiencing a fundamental shift toward the promotion of the political components of the idea, especially with the emergence of the open data phenomenon whose quick global diffusion worldwide is

Table 3.5 The international rating of the e-government project from 2003 to 2014

	Global ranking of the national e-government project						
	2003	*2004*	*2005*	*2008*	*2010*	*2012*	*2014*
Kazakhstan	83th	69th	65th	81th	46th	38th	28th

Source: elaboration based on data from UNPAN (2003, 2004, 2005, 2008, 2010, 2012, 2014)

transforming even the core of the e-government paradigm. The development of the open government concept, in this respect, is probably one of the key prospective directions to follow. This pathway will require not only changes in the traditional realm of e-government but, more important, in fundamental political transformations in the affected societies and nations. The inclination of the new concept toward advancing the political aspects of e-government development rather than promoting the traditional institutions of public administration such as civic engagement and peer-to-peer collaborative projects, which usually require completely new e-government realization strategies and tactics (Kassen, 2012), could fundamentally transform the future of the e-government concept, making it more autonomous and more independent from the direct influence of government agencies, which have traditionally played a crucial role in the process almost in every country. In this regard, further progress in advancing the concept in Kazakhstan will depend on whether the national authorities of the country admit these changes and demonstrate a political will to adopt their realization strategies to the new challenges, which would allow the nation to further the idea in new niches of this multidimensional phenomenon and hopefully harness promising political and economic benefits in the future.

References

The Adilet Open Laws Project (2015). http://adilet.zan.kz/eng

Al-Khamayseh, S., Lawrence, E., & Zmijewska, A. (2006). Towards understanding success factors in interactive mobile government. Paper presented at the Proceedings of Euro mGov 2006: The Second European Conference on Mobile Government, Brighton, UK.

Amailef, K., & Lu, J. (2013). Ontology-supported case-based reasoning approach for intelligent m-Government emergency response services. *Decision Support Systems, 55*(1), 79–97.

Arora, S. (2008). National e-ID card schemes: A European overview. *Information Security Technical Report, 13*(2), 46–53.

Åström, J., Karlsson, M., Linde, J., & Pirannejad, A. (2012). Understanding the rise of e-participation in non-democracies: Domestic and international factors. *Government Information Quarterly, 29*(2), 142–150.

Bhuiyan, S. H. (2010). E-government in Kazakhstan: Challenges and its role to development. *Public Organization Review, 10*(1), 31–47.

Bhuiyan, S. H. (2011). Trajectories of e-government implementation for public sector service delivery in Kazakhstan. *International Journal of Public Administration, 34*(9), 604–615.

CETT (2015). The Center for Engineering and Transfer of Technologies. http://www.cett.kz/

Chadwick, A., & May, C. (2003). Interaction between states and citizens in the age of the internet: "e-government" in the United States, Britain, and the European Union. *Governance-Oxford, 16*(2), 271–300.

The Committee of Transport (2015). The Committee of Transport in the Ministry of Investments and Development of Kazakhstan. http://transport.mid.gov.kz/ru

The Decree N 88-b (2005, April 5). The rules for the registration of the domain space in the Kazakhstan segment of the Internet. The decree of the Acting Chairman of the Informatization and Communication Agency of Kazakhstan.

The Directive N 464 (2013, January 8). The State Program Information Kazakhstan – 2020. http://adilet.zan.kz/rus/docs/U1300000464#z0

The Directive N 958 (2010, March 19). The Forced Industrial and Innovation Development of Kazakhstan in 2010–2014. http://adilet.zan.kz/rus/docs/U100000958_

ECC (2015). The Electronic Commerce Center. http://ecc.kz/en

The E-Government Directive # 1471 (2004, November 10). The State Program of E-government Formation in Kazakhstan for 2005–2007 (2004). The Presidential Directive. http://adilet.zan.kz/rus/docs/U040001471_

The E-Government of Kazakhstan (2015). www.egov.kz

The E-Procurement Law (2007, July 21). N 303-III. http://adilet.zan.kz/rus/docs/Z070000303_

The Government Resolution N 1155–1 (2007, November 30). The Program of E-government Formation in Kazakhstan for 2008–2010. http://adilet.zan.kz/rus/docs/P0700011551

Harrison, T. M., Guerrero, S., Burke, G. B., Cook, M., Cresswell, A., Helbig, N., . . . Pardo, T. (2011, June). Open government and e-government: Democratic challenges from a public value perspective. In *Proceedings of the 12th Annual International Digital Government Research Conference: Digital Government Innovation in Challenging Times* (pp. 245–253). College Park, MD: ACM.

Hung, S. Y., Chang, C. M., & Kuo, S. R. (2013). User acceptance of mobile e-government services: An empirical study. *Government Information Quarterly*, *30*(1), 33–44.

IBP USA (2009). *Kazakhstan company laws and regulations handbook*. (Vol. 1). Strategic Information and Regulations. Washington, D.C.: International Business Publications.

IITU (2015). The International Information Technology University. www.iitu.kz

Janssen, M., Charalabidis, Y., & Zuiderwijk, A. (2012). Benefits, adoption barriers and myths of open data and open government. *Information Systems Management*, *29*(4), 258–268.

Kassen, M. (2010). *E-Government in Kazakhstan: Realization and prospects*, 6. Carbondale: Open SIUC, Southern Illinois University. http://opensiuc.lib.siu.edu/pnconfs_2010/6/

Kassen, M. (2012). *Empowering social media: Citizens-source e-Government and peer-to-peer networks*, 3. Carbondale: Open SIUC, Southern Illinois University. http://opensiuc.lib.siu.edu/pnconfs_2012/3/

Kassen, M. (2013). A promising phenomenon of open data: A case study of the Chicago open data project. *Government Information Quarterly*, *30*(4), 508–513.

Kazakhtelecom (2015). www.telecom.kz/en

KazPost (2015). www.kazpost.kz

KazSatNet (2015). www.kazsatnet.kz

Kushchu, I. (2007). *Mobile government: An emerging direction in e-Government*. Hershey, PA: IGI Publishing.

Kushchu, I., & Kuscu, H. (2003, July). From E-government to M-government: Facing the inevitable. In *The 3rd European Conference on E-Government* (pp. 253–260). MCIL Trinity College, Dublin, Ireland.

Lathrop, D., & Ruma, L. (2010). *Open government: Collaboration, transparency, and participation in practice.* Sebastopol, CA: O'Reilly Media, Inc.

Lee, S. M., Tan, X., & Trimi, S. (2005). Current practices of leading e-government countries. *Communications of the ACM, 48*(10), 99–104.

Linde, J., & Karlsson, M. (2013). The dictator's new clothes: The relationship between e-Participation and quality of government in non-democratic regimes. *International Journal of Public Administration, 36*(4), 269–281.

Lyon, D. (2005). The border is everywhere: ID cards, surveillance and the other. In E. Zureik & M. B. Salter (Eds.), *Global surveillance and policing: Borders, security, identity*, Vol. 5 (pp. 66–82). Portland, OR: Willan Publishing.

Lyon, D. (2009). *Identifying citizens: ID cards as surveillance.* Malden, MA: Polity Press.

McGlinchey, E., & Johnson, E. (2007). Aiding the Internet in central Asia. *Democratisation, 14*(2), 273–288.

McKenzie, R., Crompton, M., & Wallis, C. (2008). Use cases for identity management in e-government. *IEEE Security & Privacy, 6*(2), 51–57.

MIDK (2015). The Ministry of Investments and Development of Kazakhstan. http://www.mid.gov.kz/en

MJK (2015). The Ministry of Justice of Kazakhstan. www.adilet.gov.kz/en

MNEK (2015). The Ministry of the National Economy. http://economy.gov.kz/en/

Moon, M. J. (2002). The evolution of e-government among municipalities: Rhetoric or reality? *Public Administration Review, 62*(4), 424–433.

NATD (2015). The National Agency of Technological Development. http://natd.gov.kz

Obi, T., & Iwasaki, N. (Eds.). (2015). *A decade of world e-Government rankings* (Vol. 7). Amsterdam: IOS Press.

OECD (2007). *Fighting corruption in transition economies: Kazakhstan 2007.* Paris: OECD Publishing.

The Online Conference Platform (2015). http://egov.kz/wps/portal/conference?lang=ru

The Open Government Project (2015). http://open.egov.kz/

Ospanova, S. (2015, April 7). Kazakhstani postmen to be provided with smartphones. *Kazpravda Newspaper.* http://www.kazpravda.kz/en/rubric/society/kazakhstani-postmen-to-be-provided-with-smartphones/

Otjacques, B., Hitzelberger, P., & Feltz, F. (2007). Interoperability of e-government information systems: Issues of identification and data sharing. *Journal of Management Information Systems, 23*(4), 29–51.

The Public E-Procurement Project (2015). http://www.goszakup.gov.kz/

RCLI (2015). The Republican Center of Legal Information. http://www.rkao.kz

Resolution N 369 (2014, April 17). On the Agency of Informatization and communication of Kazakhstan. http://adilet.zan.kz/rus/docs/P1400000369#z12

Resolution N 479 (2005). On approval of the development of the joint-stock company Kazakhtelecom for 2005–2007. Resolution of the Government of the Republic of Kazakhstan dated May 19, 2005 N 479"

Resolution N 983 (2010, September 29). The Program of the Information and Communication Technology Development in Kazakhstan for 2010–2014. http://adilet.zan.kz/rus/docs/P100000983_

Shareef, M. A., Archer, N., & Dwivedi, Y. K. (2012). Examining adoption behavior of mobile government. *The Journal of Computer Information Systems, 53*(2), 39.

UNPAN (2003). The Global E-Government Survey. United Nations Public Administration Network. http://unpan3.un.org/egovkb/en-us/Reports/UN-E-Government-Survey-2003

UNPAN (2004). Global E-Government Readiness Report. Towards Access for Opportunity. http://unpan1.un.org/intradoc/groups/public/documents/un/unpan019207.pdf

UNPAN (2005). UN Global E-government Readiness Report. From e-Government to e-Inclusion. http://unpan1.un.org/intradoc/groups/public/documents/un/unpan021888.pdf

UNPAN (2008). UN Global E-Government Survey. From E-Government to Connected Governance. http://unpan1.un.org/intradoc/groups/public/documents/un/unpan028607.pdf

UNPAN (2010). The Global E-Government Survey. Leveraging E-government at a Time of Financial and Economic Crisis. http://www2.unpan.org/egovkb/global_reports/10report.htm

UNPAN (2012). The Global E-Government Survey. E-Government for the People. http://unpan3.un.org/egovkb/Portals/egovkb/Documents/un/2012-Survey/unpan048065.pdf

UNPAN (2014). The Global E-Government Survey. E-Government for the Future We Want. http://unpan3.un.org/egovkb/Reports/UN-E-Government-Survey-2014

Venkatesh, V., Chan, F. K., & Thong, J. Y. (2012). Designing e-government services: Key service attributes and citizens' preference structures. *Journal of Operations Management, 30*(1), 116–133.

Zerde (2015). The National Telecommunication Holding. www.zerde.gov.kz

4 A content analysis of key e-government projects in Kazakhstan

When it comes to practical aspects of promotion and implementation, the e-government concept is realized differently from country to country, exposing a plethora of national strategies and policies in the area and reflecting a multidimensional nature of the phenomenon. In Kazakhstan, because of the strong traditions of unitary governance and centralized structure of political management at all levels of public administration, e-government is regarded both politically and technologically as a universal single-entry platform for all ICT-driven initiatives in public administration at both national and local levels. Therefore, to understand fully the diffusion of the phenomenon in Kazakhstan, it is necessary to analyze in a holistic manner the development of all projects that *per se* constitute the core of the national e-government concept as a public platform for all initiatives in the sphere.

Introduction: e-government as a multi-compositional platform

In Kazakhstan, the realization of any public project that focuses on using technological aspects to reform public administration at the national and local levels is regarded as part of the state e-government strategy and almost all projects in the sphere are integrated into a single platform, which are interconnected with single government databases and even universal mechanisms of citizens' authentication (The E-Government of Kazakhstan, 2015). In general, e-government is considered by the top political leadership as a strategy of national priority, therefore, its realization is financially and technologically supported by the state budget in a systematic manner that resulted in an emergence of several e-government initiatives. Many of them proved to be popular among the citizenry. In this regard, projects such as the Electronic Application System (e-application), the Electronic Appointment System (e-appointment), the Mobile Government (m-government), the Electronic Learning (e-learning), the Electronic Licensing System (e-licensing), the Electronic Public Procurement (e-procurement), the Electronic Notary (e-notary), the Electronic Taxation (e-taxation), Electronic Payment System (e-payment) and the Public Service Centers (one-stop shops) initiatives are among the most developed.

The e-government projects in Kazakhstan: realizing the multidimensional nature of the phenomena

The E-Application Project: de-bureaucratizing public administration

The development of the E-Application Project is one of the most promising undertakings in the overall implementation of the e-government program in Kazakhstan, since the principle of its work could dramatically change the fundamentals of a somewhat cumbersome and ineffective administration system that has existed in this post-Soviet nation whose public sector is notorious for its bureaucracy at all levels of government (Rustemova, 2011). Presumably aimed at helping citizens in their official correspondence and everyday communication with government agencies, it resorts to a special digital tracking mechanism embedded in the system of public administration that could allow significant increases in the level of transparency in the sector, effectively battling both red tape and corruption. Technically, by using the service, citizens could send their electronic applications to public agencies at the national level through a single portal of e-government (The E-Application System, 2015). The main advantage of the system is allowing the applicants to track the status of their applications in real time with a guarantee that they will receive an answer or reaction from the government agencies in a timely manner (see figure 4.1).

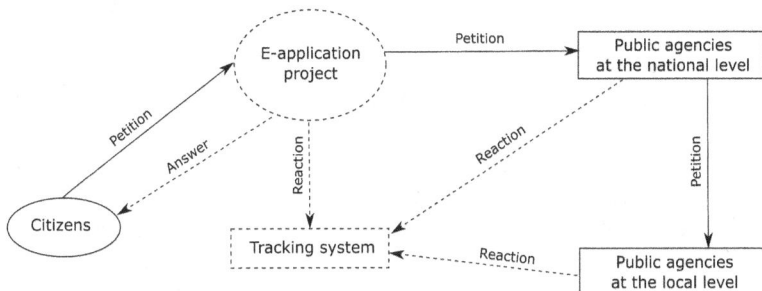

Figure 4.1 The mechanism of the E-Application Project

Source: own illustration

The new mechanism of the digital control arguably could change the traditional algorithm of operation in public administration, making it presumably more accountable. Moreover, due to automation of the application processing procedures, the E-Application Project might be regarded as one of the most important parts of the ICT-based public administration system. It could dramatically increase its efficiency by fighting red tape that has been a scourge of government agencies in Kazakhstan.

The service is available for both citizens and businesses provided they have an electronic digital signature and are registered in the portal of e-government as users. In this regard, the authentication of users is a crucial aspect of the system. The mechanism is based on a globally used technology well-known among ICT professionals as *a federated identity system* (Baldoni, 2012) or *single-sign-on system* (SSO) (De Clercq, 2002), which allows the integration of all e-service platforms with a single-entry mechanism. In this regard, one of the prominent examples of the system is the mechanism of authentication used by the Google Corporation for its various services (Ciurana, 2009).

Usually the deadline for the government agencies to react to citizens' petitions is fifteen days (The E-Government of Kazakhstan, 2015) with some exceptions for one month if it is necessary to request additional documents or information. One of the interesting aspects of the system is that all petitions and decisions of the government agencies are assigned a unique identification number for easy tracking in the system, which presumably eliminates chances of red tape in public administration, at least at the national level.

The e-procurement project: ensuring transparency in public spending

The electronic public procurement initiative (e-procurement) is one of the most interesting projects in the development of e-government in Kazakhstan, since it presumably saves significant financial resources in the public acquisition of goods and services (Kassen, 2010). Officially, the e-procurement project is a special web portal that provides a single-entry platform for all electronic public procurement transactions (The Public e-Procurement Project, 2015). Almost all government agencies at both national and local levels, as well as state-owned national corporations, are obliged to procure at the single portal of the e-procurement system.

The traditional public procurement was notoriously ineffective due to a high level of corruption and bureaucracy in the sphere. In fact, one of the main reasons to introduce the e-procurement project was a desperate attempt to settle the issue and ultimately guarantee normal functioning of the public administration system, which is unthinkable today without normal public procurement procedures (Hardy & Williams, 2008). It is especially important in Kazakhstan, since the share of government in the national economy is extremely high and the public sector is *de facto* a key player in the market. In some cases, participation in public procurement is the only way for many private companies to stay afloat.

It is necessary to mention that the reformation of public procurement was one of the most debatable and controversial topics in the overall implementation of e-government projects in Kazakhstan, since businesses were interested in increased transparency in transactions with government agencies in the sector to ensure fair competition and better conditions for all players in the market. Moreover, government authorities have always regarded the public procurement sector as a stimulating factor (Mouraviev, Kakabadse & Robinson, 2012) for the private sector to prosper on government spending as if it is an additional tool to boost the national economy through various tenders where the national producers of goods and services would be preferred over foreign providers and thus would have a competitive advantage, at least, in the domestic market. The protectionism in the domestic market, including the public procurement sphere, was one of the reasons for the country's long journey toward the World Trade Organization (WTO) (Hindley, 2008), the accession to which were finalized only in 2015 after almost two decades of negotiations and hesitation. In this regard, it is interesting to note that, according to Kjærnet et al. (2008), there is a strong relationship between business and political groups in Kazakhstan, which results in strong lobbying from the former in the sphere, too.

Technically, the principle of the e-procurement project is straightforward. The main purpose of the initiative is to guarantee the best price for the procured goods and services, providing transparency of electronic transactions for businesses that participate in the auctions and presumably ensuring the protection of public interests in controlling the fulfillment of the procurement orders after the electronic tenders.

Therefore, to participate in the electronic tenders, the potential vendors should register in the e-procurement portal by using the digital signature identification. Another function of the system is to provide free public access to various statistical data and reports on current and completed tenders as well as the government plans on future orders to ensure better transparency and public scrutiny of the entire process. It also provides text and video guides for potential vendors on how to participate in the system and publishes all legal acts that regulate the sphere.

Officially, the purpose of the e-procurement project is to save public funds that are spent on the acquisition of goods and services ordered by government agencies as well as on the organization of the procurement procedures, provide a universal platform for all electronic tenders for the public sector at both national and local levels, create a healthy competitive environment in the market, ensure free public access to all information related to public procurement in electronic form, decrease the volume of paperwork in government agencies, and finally battle corruption in the sphere due to better transparency of the system (The Public e-Procurement Project, 2015).

The E-Appointment Platform: e-bureaucracy again?

The E-Appointment Project might be regarded as an additional tool aimed at providing better efficiency of the whole public administration system since the purpose of the initiative is to create a digital platform that would track all online appointments of top government officials with citizens and businesses (Kassen, 2014), presumably to increase the openness of government agencies and make them more accessible to people. For example, to make an online appointment with a minister or governor, citizens should register in the system and then choose an appropriate date and time for the online conference (The E-Appointment System, 2015). However, after receiving an e-mail confirmation, they have to visit a nearby Public Service Center for the video conference, which again requires a physical presence, waiting in lines, additional registration, identification, checking, etc., eventually turning a presumably promising project into an additionally expensive, time-consuming and non-effective e-bureaucracy platform (see figure 4.2).

The E-Licensing Project: digitizing the licensing business

The E-Licensing Project is another e-government system aimed at the informatization of all licensing and government permission procedures

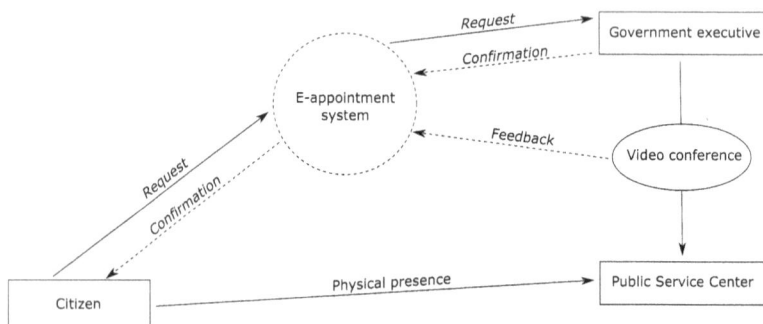

Figure 4.2 The E-Appointment Project as a poster child of e-bureaucracy
Source: own illustration

in Kazakhstan. Created and launched in 2008, the main beneficiary of the project is a business sector that is usually interested in the elimination of any barriers in applying to licenses issued by various government agencies (Chesbrough, 2010). The services that the system provides are among the most popular for businesses, since all permission documents and licenses are issued in an electronic form and stored in a single database at both national and local levels. Therefore, the service is of special interest for business people living in remote areas of Kazakhstan who find it difficult to visit physically the government licensors due to huge distances of the country and lack of good roads.

The key advantage of the electronic system is that it dramatically increases the quality of transactions between government and businesses due to automation and streamlining of licensing processes. In fact, to receive licenses or register a firm, businesspeople do not need to have a lot of documents at their disposal at the moment of application which had been required until recently. This measure could potentially decrease chances for the emergence of corruption and red tape in the sphere by replacing the traditional middleman in the process with an automated proxy platform that controls and tracks all steps of registration and issues the documents. Moreover, the project also allows checking through the web portal the authenticity of any licenses and permissions documents issued previously by the system, reducing the possibility of document forgery in the area.

The e-licensing platform receives applications to issue permits in the following categories: security, natural monopolies, protection of competition in the market, health, land cadastre, imports and exports, culture, telecommunications, education, environmental protection, industry and technology, agriculture, construction business, transport and finances. In this respect, applications from businesses to receive government permits for construction and installation works, medical and educational activities and for the sale of alcoholic beverages are among the most popular requests (The E-Licensing Project, 2015).

It is necessary to note the development of the e-licensing initiative could be regarded as one of the most successful aspects in the overall realization of the e-government program in Kazakhstan since, according to Reddick and Roy (2013), the development of e-services that help businesses to prosper could dramatically increase the satisfaction of people with e-government. The successful implementation of the project has recently received positive reviews of the international experts in the e-government sphere. For example, during the World Summit on the Information Society in May 2013, the system was recognized as the best solution in the e-business category in the world, according to the WSIS global contest (The International Telecommunication Union, 2015).

The E-Payment Platform: creating a public e-commerce system

Even though some of the e-government services are fee-based, both for businesses and citizens, the E-Payment Project is mostly a business-oriented platform aimed at providing commercial organizations with a universal electronic payment venue (The E-Payment Project, 2015). The ultimate goal is to simplify and track easily all financial transactions between government agencies and the private sector, since nearly all payments for e-government services for businesses and citizens are integrated and processed through the e-payment system. The Ministry of Finance provides political support for the project while the platform is closely connected with the payment system of one of the commercial banks. In order to make government payments, citizens or businesses should register an account in the system and have a debit or credit card. In addition, the project could be used as a venue to confirm payments for e-government services and transactions that citizens receive directly from the Public Service Centers.

The popularity of the e-payment transactions through the project demonstrates a dramatic increase from the total of 3 billion KZT in 2014 to 6 billion KZT (approximately 32 million USD), as of August 2015, only for the first eight months of 2015 (Kazinform, 2015b). In this regard, the most popular e-payments that are processed through the platform are payments for various fee-based e-government services, fines for traffic-related offenses, payments for licenses and permits, custom duties, payments for public utilities, government fees for financial operations with real property, etc. (The E-Government of Kazakhstan, 2015). There are plans to integrate the platform with private e-payment systems so that citizens and businesses would have an opportunity to pay both government and commercial services through one venue (The E-Government of Kazakhstan, 2015). It would presumably help government authorities to track all financial transactions in the market, improving the information security of the e-commerce sector against misuse and frauds in the area because of better public control.

The E-Taxation System: simplifying tax reporting

The E-Taxation Project is another e-government project aimed at simplifying financial transactions related to taxation between citizens, businesses and government agencies. This measure presumably helps to battle red tape and create fewer opportunities for the emergence of corruption in the area since citizens and businesses could dramatically decrease the level of physical contact with government agents, using the system for online tax reporting. The key advantage of the system is that people could interact with the Kazakh Internal Revenue Service (IRS) through the system since nearly all transactions of both bureaucratic and financial nature could be processed online. It is necessary to note that in Kazakhstan the majority of taxes are flat rate, which eases the process of automation while the regulation rules and instructions in the sphere are simple and comprehensible because of the unitary nature of the public administration system.

Technically, the project allows taxpayers to create a special account in the system where they can fill in all forms online and electronically send them to the Kazakh IRS (The E-Taxation Project, 2015). In order to secure the transactions, all completed forms are processed through the mechanism of electronic digital signatures. In addition, taxpayers could use the system to track the status of sent tax forms and all related transactions with government agencies, view reports and send feedback on how to improve the mechanism of the E-Taxation Project, improve the interface of the platform, etc.

It is necessary to note that all transactions are processed using the encryption systems that are practiced in the Internet banking sphere. Therefore, the project does not provide any client-based computer application and all operations are made online through web browsers using a universal standard method of encryption such as the secure sockets layer technology (SSL), which provides a decent security connection (Kahate, 2013), for example, between the web server of the IRS server and the taxpayer's browser. In addition, the e-taxation portal offers text and video guides on how users can use the system more effectively. Although Kazakh tax law is simple and unambiguous, some areas of the taxation legislation might be labyrinthine, especially for small businesses and joint ventures. In this regard, the portal provides more detailed instructions and interactive tools to familiarize taxpayers with other system options.

The Public Service Centers: the Kazakh version of one-stop shops

The Public Service Centers (PSCs) or one-stop shop (OSS) project is one of the most successfully realized e-government projects in Kazakhstan (Knox, 2008; Janenova, 2009; Bhuiyan, 2010). In fact, the diffusion of hundreds of centers all over the country is evidence of success in the area (The Public Service Centers Project, 2015). The main idea of the project is to provide citizens, who are not familiar with ICTs or could not afford to work with computers due to various reasons, an opportunity to receive government e-services and enjoy other options that the e-government projects offer online through the special centers that are directly connected with all government-based servers and databases.

Moreover, some government services could be provided only through the PSCs, especially those that require the physical presence of the petitioner – e.g.

in order to receive the national IDs, driver's licenses or passports that had been previously ordered online through the e-government portal since the identification documents could not be sent by post for security reasons. Another example is when citizens need to receive the digital signatures instruments to harness fully the interactive potential of the e-government projects. The instruments could be issued by government only through the centers. In this respect, the PSCs play a crucial role of being a focal point for many government-related operations.

For people living in the countryside, in many cases it is the only way to interact with national authorities by participating in the Internet conferences with top executives without living in their villages or small towns. In this regard, the PSCs are one of the most popular public places where people not only could receive various government services but also know the latest news and talk with other people. Many centers are situated in residential areas and often provide complimentary services such as consultations and free Wi-Fi. Therefore, the centers contribute to the social networking of people, especially at the local level.

It is necessary to note there are two types of PSCs: one is for the general population and the second one is specialized centers for drivers.

The specialized centers provide all services that are related to the road police activity such as issuing driver's licenses, testing drivers, providing medical examinations, registering new cars, paying custom duties, etc. (The Public Service Centers Project, 2015). Another difference from the general centers is that almost all services there are provided on a fee basis. Technically, the specialized centers provide all spectra of services related to the transportation area. The driver's test is carried out at the special examination site that is fully equipped with the latest technological tools and cameras to track any actions and movements of the future driver. The automated method of examination is designed to decrease to a minimum any interactions between applicants and government agents.

The E-Learning Project: digitizing education or building infrastructure?

The E-Learning Project is a specialized e-government platform aimed at providing citizens and businesses with all public services related to the secondary education sphere from one venue. Officially, the E-Learning Project is focused on improving the standards of secondary education through the introduction and wide use of various technological platforms in public schools across the country (The E-Learning Project, 2015). In this regard, the national authorities pay special attention to the project and provide solid funding for its implementation in educational institutions. For example, in

2011 almost one billion US dollars were given by the state budget for its realization (Tengrinews, 2011), making it one of the most expensive ICT-driven projects not only in the e-government sphere but also in the whole public administration sector. One of the reasons for the huge government spending is the need to update the infrastructural basis of the public schools – e.g. the procurement of computer equipment and provision of the broad-band Internet access as well as the development of computer software for various e-education platforms and systems.

The main target audience of the project is a wide range of various public and private organizations that provide educational services such as lyceums, schools and training centers, as well as an army of students and their parents is. Moreover, the ample public funding of the projects and the necessity to procure a huge volume of goods and services such as personal computers, laptops and tablets, interactive billboards, satellite equipment, etc., as well as a wide range of software and installation services, drew interest from various ICT companies both state-owned and private ones.

According to the portal of the project, the benefits of the e-learning system are confined to the opportunities that it offers for teachers, students, parents and school administrators (The E-Learning Project, 2015). For example, teachers could use the system to grade their students and track school results, organize online conferences and webinars with students, communicate with students' parents online, make various reports to school administrators, etc. Students could use the platform to receive online homework tasks and assignments from schoolteachers, receive alerts of any changes in the syllabus or schedule of classes, download electronic textbooks and dictionaries, track grades in the electronic journal, etc. For parents, the project offers more effective opportunities to track the progress of their children in the school, watch online the class activities in real time, communicate with teachers and school administrators, etc. Administrators can benefit from the system by automating school activities such as class scheduling, reporting on students' progress, communicating with parents and teachers, organizing e-libraries, developing test programs, etc.

The mobile e-government project: following the global trend

The main purpose of the Mobile Government Project is to develop a platform that would offer some of the e-government services via mobile devices such as smartphones and tablet computers. The recent trend in the diffusion of various handheld digital devices and rapid growth of the market in Kazakhstan makes the administrators of the e-government program pay attention to the sector, too. In this regard, at the moment the project offers two versions of the e-government application in Apple Store and Google

Play (The Mobile Government of Kazakhstan, 2015), taking into account the popularity of the iOS and Android mobile operating systems. A wide range of e-government services are provided by the application. For example, it is possible to receive information on all registered real properties, pay fines for traffic violations, subscribe for various alerts from government agencies, etc. In addition, by installing the mobile version of the digital signature certificate, citizens can also receive interactive services such as the issue of birth and marriage certificates, address certificates, pay custom duties, etc. In general, the mobile e-government application provides more than fifty e-services for citizens of Kazakhstan. Looking at the users' approval rating provided by Google Play, one can see that in general two thirds of the feedback is in favor of the application.

The E-Notary Project: digitizing the notary business

The single notary information system, or E-Notary Project, is another e-government project that provides a single-entry venue for all notaries registered in Kazakhstan which regulates their interaction with the national notary chambers and the Ministry of Justice. One of the purposes of the project is to ensure higher accountability and transparency of the notary business in the country through the integration with available registries and databases in the sphere; therefore, it is primarily a G2B platform. However, the project might be interesting for citizens by providing some information services such as access to the database by all notaries, checking the flat tariffs for the notary services, etc. (The E-Notary Project, 2015).

References

Baldoni, R. (2012). Federated identity management systems in e-government: The case of Italy. *Electronic Government, an International Journal*, *9*(1), 64–84.

Bhuiyan, S. H. (2010). E-government in Kazakhstan: Challenges and its role to development. *Public Organization Review*, *10*(1), 31–47.

Chesbrough, H. (2010). Business model innovation: Opportunities and barriers. *Long Range Planning*, *43*(2), 354–363.

Ciurana, E. (2009). *Developing with google app engine*. New York: Apress.

De Clercq, J. (2002). Single sign-on architectures. In G. I. Davida, Y. Frankel & O. Rees (Eds.), *Infrastructure security* (pp. 40–58). Berlin Heidelberg: Springer.

The E-application System (2015). http://egov.kz/wps/portal/Content?contentPath=/egovcontent/citizensgovernment/articlesforcg/passport/e_app&lang=ru

The E-Appointment System (2015). http://egov.kz/wps/portal/Content?content Path=/egovcontent/citizensgovernment/articlesforcg/passport/online_admi ssion&lang=ena

The E-Government of Kazakhstan (2015). www.egov.kz

The E-Learning Project (2015). http://e.edu.kz
The E-Licensing Project (2015). http://elicense.kz
The E-Notary Project (2015). http://enis.kz
The E-Payment Project (2015). www.epay.gov.kz
The E-Taxation Project (2015). http://cabinet.salyk.kz
Hardy, C. A., & Williams, S. P. (2008). E-government policy and practice: A theoretical and empirical exploration of public e-procurement. *Government Information Quarterly*, *25*(2), 155–180.
Hindley, B. (2008). *Kazakhstan and the world economy: An assessment of Kazakhstan's trade policy and pending accession to the WTO*. Brussels: European Centre for International Political Economy.
The International Telecommunication Union (2015). https://itunews.itu.int/En/3946-Electronic-licensing-in-Kazakhstan.note.aspx
Janenova, S. (2009). One stop shop in Kazakhstan: Breaking-up traditional bureaucracy or a new look for old practice. In *Open Society Institute/Local Government Initiative Fellowship, Conference Paper*.
Kahate, A. (2013). *Cryptography and network security*. New Delhi: Tata McGraw-Hill Education.
Kassen, M. (2010). *E-Government in Kazakhstan: Realization and prospects*, 6. Carbondale: Open SIUC, Southern Illinois University. http://opensiuc.lib.siu.edu/pnconfs_2010/6/
Kassen, M. (2014). Globalization of e-government: Open government as a global agenda; benefits, limitations and ways forward. *Information Development*, *30*(1), 51–58.
Kazinform (2015). http://www.inform.kz/rus/article/2818035
Kjærnet, H., Satpaev, D., & Torjesen, S. (2008, February). Big business and high-level politics in Kazakhstan: An everlasting symbiosis? *The China and Eurasia Forum Quarterly*, *6*(1), 95–107.
Knox, C. (2008). Kazakhstan: Modernizing government in the context of political inertia. *International Review of Administrative Sciences*, *74*(3), 477–496.
The Mobile Government of Kazakhstan (2015). http://egov.kz/wps/portal/Content?contentPath=/egovcontent/transports/communications/article/mobile_goverment&lang=ru
Mouraviev, N., Kakabadse, N., & Robinson, I. (2012). Concessionary nature of public-private partnerships in Russia and Kazakhstan: A critical review. *International Journal of Public Administration*, *35*(6), 410–420.
The Public E-Procurement Project (2015). http://www.goszakup.gov.kz/
The Public Service Centers Project (2015). http://con.gov.kz/
Reddick, C. G., & Roy, J. (2013). Business perceptions and satisfaction with e-government: Findings from a Canadian survey. *Government Information Quarterly*, *30*(1), 1–9.
Rustemova, A. (2011). Political economy of Central Asia: Initial reflections on the need for a new approach. *Journal of Eurasian Studies*, *2*(1), 30–39.
Tengrinews (2011). http://en.tengrinews.kz/edu/Almost-1-billion-allocated-for-e-learning-in-Kazakhstan-4092/

5 Open government in Kazakhstan

A tentative touch of participative democracy?

This chapter of the book is dedicated to policy analysis of public initiatives and projects aimed at developing new dimensions of the e-government concept in Kazakhstan, such as open government and open data, in an attempt to understand the political motivations of national authorities to promote such projects and answer the ultimate question of the research whether they advance digital democracy and civic engagement or it is merely a demonstration of the mighty administrative and financial capability of the central government to launch, support and effectively manipulate such presumably e-democracy-focused platforms that have nothing to do with the development of democratic institutions and the political reality is hidden by the stalking horse of e-transparency. In addition, this chapter claims to be agenda-setting research since the author will also try to offer recommendations for Kazakh political leaders and e-government practitioners on what areas of the open government concept they should first concentrate their activities in the ICT-driven public sector reforms and explain why the traditional and arguably effective thus far administrative methods of the e-government promotion will no longer work when entering the open government realm. The recommendations of the research can be extrapolated to the political leadership in almost any developing country in the world and could be interesting for researchers who investigate the concept in their future studies and hypothesis testing.

Introduction: is open government a reincarnation of e-government?

Open government has recently become a watchword of ICT-driven public administration reforms in many countries worldwide, arguably providing a new conceptual paradigm to revise a once popular but somewhat forgotten idea of e-government (Google Trends, 2015) into a new political domain where attributes of democracy such as civic engagement and political participation are possible to implement in practice as never before due to a promising phenomenon of transparency and collaboration created in societies that once adopted the concept. However, in researching available literature on the topic, the case studies are mostly focused on the most developed countries of the world with longstanding traditions of transparency in government and established democratic institutions – i.e. political values that are universally regarded in academia as necessary prerequisites for the concept to be fully realized. In this regard, it seems logical to analyze the development of the open government technology in a typical developing nation and understand whether and how it can change the traditional channels of political communication there. In this respect, Kazakhstan is an interesting candidate for the case study, since being a relatively young nation that received its independence only two decades ago, it has already been recognized as a poster child of the great economic opportunities that e-government may offer in reforming the public sector in a typical emerging country but leaving many questions about the implications of the reforms in a political domain.

Building a framework for policy analysis

Learning the research background

Although the development of e-government (Knox, 2008; Bhuiyan, 2010; Janenova, 2010; Johnson & Kolko, 2010; Kassen, 2010; Bhuiyan, 2011) and ICT-driven public administration in Kazakhstan (Verheijen, 2007; Bhuiyan & Amagoh, 2011; Bhuiyan, 2011b) is a popular topic in scientific literature, the open government agenda in Kazakhstan is a new research direction due to the infancy of the concept itself and there is no academic material in the area. However, the open government idea is actively implemented today in Kazakhstan under global influence since political leaders all over the world are beginning to regard it as a modern interpretation of e-government and even as a political platform to further e-democracy, at least from a formal point of view. In this regard, in Kazakhstan the realization of the open government concept is also viewed as an important indicator of progress and as a unique benchmark in assessing the overall e-government readiness, which eventually could help improve the international image of the country. Therefore, the concept is more popular among e-government policy makers and practitioners (The E-Government of Kazakhstan, 2015) and related professional audiences such as NGOs (Internews Kazakhstan, 2015; Soros Foundation, 2015) and ICT developers (NITEC, 2015) rather than in academia.

Setting the research methodology

Considering that the topic is new in Kazakhstan, the case study of the open government projects seems to be the most appropriate research method since it could provide an empirical playground to further the theoretical analysis in future investigations. In this regard, the study will heavily rely on the analysis of interpretive data, which generally consists of observations, including the observation of the official open data web portals and related open data-driven projects, analysis of contextual data such as legislation and executive acts, analysis of online communication networks between key stakeholders of the project – i.e. policy makers, ICT developers, NGOs, citizens, etc. – and in the end analysis of the statistical data provided by the central executive bodies.

Understanding the incentives for the adoption of open government in Kazakhstan

Following the global trend or just global PR?

The globalization of the open government concept worldwide due to the international efforts of the Open Government Partnership (OGP) is one of the primary reasons why the open government agenda (Kassen, 2014) is becoming a popular idea in furthering public sector reforms in many developed and developing nations, including in Kazakhstan. The OGP was created in 2011 to provide an international venue for the promotion of e-government as a universal instrument to make governments open by popularizing public values of the concept such as transparency and collaboration. Today, many developed and developing countries joined the partnership, increasing the number of member states from eight to sixty-five nations (The Open Government Partnership, 2015). Some regional neighbors of Kazakhstan such as Mongolia, Ukraine, Azerbaijan, Georgia, and Turkey have already joined the global initiative.

All these member states have taken some political commitments to improve public administration (Schwegmann, 2013) and promised to provide more transparency ICT-driven tools (Davies & Bawa, 2012) that would create a favorable atmosphere for better dialogue and communication between civil society and government. Such tools presumably can be found in the promotion of civic engagement and e-participation platforms (Evans & Campos, 2013). In this regard, the possible joining of Kazakhstan to the partnership in the near future could be regarded as a matter of prestige, too, as an indication and recognition of its achievements in building modern e-government and formal declaration of aspirations toward digital democracy in the international arena. Therefore, the national government pays special attention to the realization of the concept, considering it to be part of the e-government building plan (The Directive N 464, 2013). Any efforts to further the idea in Kazakhstan are regarded as beneficial and thus politically and financially are expected to be supported by the government.

Domestic incentives: political and economic motives

Political incentives

Another reason behind the mere desire of the national authorities to implement the open government platforms in Kazakhstan is a great opportunity that the concept could offer in the political and economic domains in building trust and confidence among citizenry and nongovernmental sectors through ICT-driven public administration platforms and techniques. After all, any innovations in the sphere, including open government, mobile government or m-government, smart government, etc., are widely regarded by the policy makers in Kazakhstan as part of the traditional e-government ecosystem, or at least in its modern interpretations, which are all arguably aimed at building trust between the state and its citizens – i.e. in the case of Kazakhstan as an additional tool to ease potential social and economic tensions in the future.

The social conflicts in neighboring countries – e.g. Georgia, Kyrgyzstan and Ukraine – that happened in recent years, partly due to the lack of public confidence in government, make authorities rethink the entire concept of public administration and welcome any ideas that would help to reform it but with one condition, it should not change the fundamentals of the political system, even if they are sometimes just cosmetic and superficial. The multidimensional public sector reforms aimed at creating presumably more professional and merit-based public administration, multiple anti-corruption measures and public hearings that are demonstratively covered by media sporadically from time to time and ostensibly the sincere desire of the leadership to make the government not only more effective but also more flexible and adaptive to the external and domestic factors, including in the ICT sphere, are all aimed at achieving the primary goal to maintain the political status quo for as long as possible.

Economic incentives

Furthermore, the political leadership sees some economic incentives in developing the open government idea in Kazakhstan, which could, in turn, strengthen the domestic political support for the government leadership. For example, by demonstrating some formal achievements in building effective and transparent e-government systems, the national authorities sincerely hope to improve the business and investment climate in the country. In addition, the development of e-government is regarded as part of important state-run programs aimed at improving modern infrastructure. For instance, the lion's share of money allocated by the national budget for the implementation of e-government from 2004 to 2007 was spent to build the national ICT infrastructure for the public sector (The e-Government Directive # 1471, 2004) – e.g. buying new computers, data servers, internet gateways, etc.

Therefore, the development of the e-government program has helped to accelerate the infrastructural readiness of the country during that period. The diffusion of broadband and fiber optic Internet, computerization of public administration, e-voting, and electronic document flow have an indirect relationship to the development of e-government in Kazakhstan.

Three-dimensional open government in Kazakhstan

Officially, the government of Kazakhstan inaugurated its open government project in 2013 with the launch of the open data portal (The open data project, 2013). The main idea of the project was to provide an effective platform for the promotion of transparency in government and increase in civic engagement. However, as an important part of the e-government realization plan, the open government concept was not limited only to open data but also included some other dimensions of the ICT-driven public sector reforms such as formal e-participation and public dialogue platforms (The Open Government Project, 2015).

Officially, among the key objectives of the open government project were the promotion of transparency, participation and collaboration in public administration – i.e. the goals that had been originally proclaimed by the Obama administration as the main pillars of the concept in his well-known open government memorandum (Obama, 2009). In general, the overall realization of the concept in Kazakhstan has been greatly influenced by the implementation of similar projects in some Western nations, especially in promoting the open data projects in the United States, Australia and Canada. However, in many developed countries, the idea of open government is regarded more as a political strategy that presumably implies multidimensional transformation in many spheres beginning from the promotion of transparency in politics and public spending and ending at the advancement of public-private partnerships. In Kazakhstan, it is mostly an instrument of the ICT-driven reforms in public administration. Therefore, its realization is similar to the development of e-government projects with the same straightforward mechanism of administrative commands, set of tools, developers, and even technological platforms paying special attention to the universal technical benchmarks and details in the sphere, such as the presence of related portals, publication of databases, PR campaigns, etc.

In this regard, when analyzing the operation of the open government project in Kazakhstan, it seems that the policy makers in the sphere adopted an interesting model of concept promotion, which could be tentatively called *a three-dimensional model of open government*. For example, the open data project, open lawmaking and open dialogue portals are the main components of the same technological platform and could be regarded as three key pillars of the concept. Each of the projects has its own mechanisms and tools of realization (see figure 5.1).

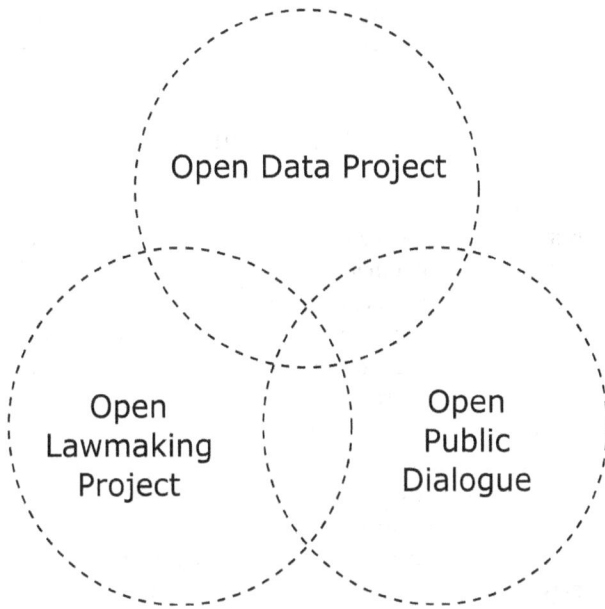

Figure 5.1 The three key components of the open government concept in Kazakhstan
Source: own illustration

The open lawmaking project: engaging or playing with the public?

Officially, the open lawmaking project (OLP) is one of three main projects aimed at ensuring a greater responsiveness and transparency of government to citizens through the opportunity to participate in the lawmaking process (The Open Lawmaking Platform, 2015). It is necessary to note that the project itself doesn't duplicate the functions of the Adilet Project that was launched in late 2013 by the government of Kazakhstan to ensure free-of-charge access of citizens and businesses to the existing legal acts through one official single-entry web resource (The Adilet Open Laws Project, 2015). The main purpose of the open lawmaking project is to presumably engage the members of the civil society to the legislative process through ICT.

In this regard, there are three guiding principles that have been declared by the administrators of the initiative in implementing the project such as the openness of the regulatory legal acts (e.g. ensuring free access to existing laws and other legal acts that has some connection to the bills under

consideration in all legislative bodies), interactive feedback and communication with citizens (e.g. voting and open commentaries on current bills),
civic engagement (e.g. PR activity through mass media to engage citizens in
the lawmaking process at the national level), and transparency of the entire
development processes through various reporting mechanisms and public
hearings (The Open Lawmaking Platform, 2015).

One of the interesting features of the project is the option to subscribe
via RSS to comments from lawyers, businesses, and government agents
and other users so that people have the opportunity to observe and track the
lawmaking process in an automatic mode in accordance with the categories
of bills and reports under consideration. In this regard, the project allows for
the discussion of categories of bills such as information technology, citizenship, family, education, career and employment, social security, citizenship,
migration and immigration, real estate, tax and finance, legal assistance,
tourism and sports, military registration and security, agriculture, licensing
and accreditation, transport and communications, health, natural resources
and ecology, intellectual property, etc.

However, it is necessary to note that the results of the comments and
discussions on the bills under consideration are not binding for the government agencies in developing the legal acts – i.e. they are merely recommendations. Therefore, it seems too arguable to say that the main idea of
the project is to increase transparency of government processes, since the
realization of the concept resembles the traditional implementation of public hearings in the area but in an online manner, which alone does not necessarily guarantee political dividends to the public administrators if there is
no clear evidence that it creates public value for the society (Wang & Wan
Wart, 2007).

Another interesting feature of the project is an opportunity to track the
history of the bills and analyze statistical data on participation and overall
activity of citizens, lawyers and other peers in the sphere in accordance
with the category of the bills. For example, the Ministry of Investments
and Development and the Ministry of Agriculture are the most active government agencies that systematically publish open bills. In general, the
platform is juristically supported by the Prosecutor General's Office, the
Ministry of Justice and the Supreme Court of Kazakhstan.

The texts of the bills are accessible through the electronic digital signature and are usually open for public hearings and discussions for one
month, which is deemed a presumably enough period of time for the public to familiarize and react accordingly to the potentially new legal acts.
The public reaction is understood as an opportunity for citizens and legal
entities to participate in discussions and vote for or against particular bills
(The Open Lawmaking Platform, 2015). In addition, the registered users

can leave comments and feedback related to the general operation of the platform. However, after analyzing the statistics of online activities of the public, the numbers are modest. For instance, although there are some documents that cause intense public debates and discussions, especially in controversial areas such as the regulation of the energy sector and social security, the majority of bills are ignored by citizens and other players of the nongovernmental sectors such as businesses, lawyers and interest groups while the average number of visitations for one bill is limited to thirty to forty views per month.

The open dialogue project: one more tool of public PR?

The Open Dialogue Project is aimed at establishing new public communication channels between the state and its citizens through two main civic engagement projects such as the official blog platform for executives of the government agencies and the Internet-conference platform.

The official blog platform

The main objective of the official blog platform of the top government executives is to make the work of public agencies more transparent and accountable to citizens by providing an opportunity to appeal directly to the heads of the ministries, bypassing traditional barriers associated with related administrative procedures by posting petitions in the blog platform (The Official Blog-Platform of Government Executives, 2015). The platform, which has already published about 300,000 posts, is extremely popular among citizens of Kazakhstan. For example, by analyzing the information on the related activity of the public available at the portal, the following types of interaction are the most popular among people:

- participation in various public discussions and debates;
- dissatisfaction with certain government officials, administrators or civil servants;
- reports on injustices and problems in communicating with local authorities or businesses;
- reports on violations of the law.

In this regard, the most popular topics lie in the following categories: information and communication technologies, mortgages, culture and information, religion, employment, health, small and medium businesses, youth policy, science, education, etc. One useful feature of the project is that all posts in the blog platform are registered with a special tracking number and assigned to a certain head of the executive body for corresponding reaction. Another measure is related to authentication and alerts, which is supplemented with the SMS verification step.

Another more important goal of the blog platform is related to image making, by helping the heads of the central government agencies to be aware of public concerns in society, since they are interested in maintaining social stability and status quo and the project is generally used as a campaign of government leadership to support its legitimacy. Many ministers and heads of departments begin to consider the platform as an additional tool of PR, since mass media tend to resort to the data available on the portal in journalistic materials. Every executive head has an official personal page on the platform where they publish not only the posts from citizens, answers and executive decisions but also hyperlinks to the accounts in popular social media platforms such as Facebook, Twitter, Vkontakte and Google Plus to ensure additional channels of communication with the public. The personal pages are apparently standardized and controlled by the central government. It is interesting to note that the concept of the blog platforms is beginning to diffuse not only at the central level of government but also at the regional one, since the same projects have been recently launched in some provinces of Kazakhstan, such as Kostanay (The Official Blog-Platform in the Kostanay Region, 2015) and the Pavlodar regions (The Official Blog-Platform in the Pavlodar Region, 2015).

The Internet-conference platform

It is necessary to note that the Internet-conference platform was launched in 2008, at the dawn of e-government development in Kazakhstan to provide an additional tool to enhance the vertical vector of political communication between the heads of the central and local executive agencies – e.g. ministries, departments and local governorships and municipalities (*akimats* in Kazakh). However, the mechanism itself had been developed even earlier. In fact, the first Internet conference was organized in 2007 with the participation of President Nursultan Nazarbayev (Ak Orda, 2007; Reuters, 2007). Later on, it became a tradition when many top members of the central government, especially prime ministers and ministers, began to take part in similar online conferences, diffusing the practice in all instances at both central and local levels. The practice was institutionalized later in the Internet-conference platform within the framework of the e-government portal. It is interesting to note that there is no law that intrinsically requires the government executives to participate in the platform. In this regard, the demonstrational example by the head of the state and prime ministers has played a key political role in the diffusion of the practice and mere political advice from the top was pretty much enough for the subordinates to follow it.

Today, the Internet-conference platform is more a PR media event than an instrument of administrative control as it was only a few years ago. The policy makers are beginning to understand that the related media coverage of the conferences, for example, between the heads of central and local government agencies, is crucial nowadays to ensure survival and continuous support of the current political system and the national authorities pay special attention to new collaborative methods of interaction with media through such platforms. Therefore, such events are usually transmitted through the central television. The administrators of the platform usually publish in advance the topic of the conference in mass media and provide technological support in launching a dedicated web page. Citizens and businesses have free access to the thread and have an option to ask questions or leave comments or complaints. Every question or comment is assigned a unique identification number for easy tracking. The special system also tracks the number of questions, answers to the questions and other statistical data to ensure administrative control (The Internet-conference platform, 2015). The media coverage of the event plays a key role, since the conference is broadcasted live on television and online in social media accounts such as Kaztube or YouTube, expanding dramatically the number of viewers. In addition, all threads are archived in the system and always freely accessible.

The open data platform: only declaring its key principles?

The open data platform is one more project that might be regarded as a key part of the open government concept in Kazakhstan. Officially, the project is aimed at making the government more transparent and accessible to citizens and businesses through the publication of open government data sets in a machine-readable format (The Open Government Project, 2015). Conceptually, the main idea of open data is to provide the nongovernmental sector with information that could later be used as raw material in third-party open-data driven projects and applications, especially at the level of municipalities and counties (Jäppinen, Toivonen & Salonen, 2013; Kassen, 2013). In this respect, civic engagement and electronic participation should play a crucial role in the overall diffusion of the concept. When analyzing the realization of the official open data project, it is necessary to mention that there are five basic principles of the concept that are pursued by policy makers in Kazakhstan such as accessibility, relevance, development of interest, authenticity and user friendliness (The Open Government Project, 2015).

All these principles could be regarded as globally universal and found in any charter documents of open data projects proclaimed by the national authorities in many countries. In fact, they should be regarded today as a reflection of the further development of the three classic principles of the open government concept such as transparency, collaboration and participation. They are all originated from the cognominal memorandum adopted by the Barack Obama administration shortly after his inauguration as president of the Unites States in early 2009. Later, the diffusion of the open data concept in the United States at the federal and local levels, and eventually all over the world, made these basic principles of open government universal.

According to the portal of the open government project, the *accessibility* implies the provision of free access to open government data without any copyright restrictions (The Open Government Project, 2015), which is important, since the material is presumably used in the creation and development of other third-party applications. The principle is closely associated with the idea of transparency that is actively promoted today worldwide by the Open Government Partnership. However, the idea is understood by the government of Kazakhstan more as a technological component of the concept rather than a political one, since the publication of open data does not necessarily lead to transparency of government, which according to Janssen et al. (2012) is one of the fundamental misunderstandings of the concept, especially among practitioners.

The *relevance* implies the provision in a timely manner of the most significant government data from various public agencies and even national companies (The Open Government Project, 2015). It is important, since in Kazakhstan the role of the central government and the national budget funds in the development of the commercial sector is extremely strong and ubiquitous. For example, the opportunity to participate in public procurement is crucial for the survival of many private companies and enterprises, taking into account the small scale of the national economy and local market niches. Many businesses are simply uncompetitive in the global market and rely heavily on harsh protective measures imposed by the national authorities on the import of goods and services and harness fully the opportunity to participate in serving a large government apparatus and public administration system through the ubiquitous instrument of public procurement. Furthermore, many large enterprises are quasi-private since the government share in some of them could reach up to 100 percent. Therefore, many state-run companies and holdings should be regarded *de facto* as part of government and could, therefore, participate in the development of the single open government project, by publishing their data sets in the data portal. In this regard, the principle of relevance includes the following categories of information that are deemed to play the most important role in gathering the data sets from both government agencies and quasi-state companies: statistical data, social welfare data and mapping data.

The *development of interest* is also regarded by the open data projects policy makers as one of the most important aspects in advancing the concept in

Kazakhstan (The Open Government Project, 2015). The launch of the open data portal is just a platform that could potentially help to increase the transparency of government, the realization of which, however, could be pointless if there are no policies on how to promote further the concept in the nongovernment sector. It is important that the administrators clearly realize the crucial role of civic engagement in this regard and understand that the successful development of the open data platform significantly depends on the activity of citizens in generating additional material in the open data-driven projects. Therefore, the development of interest among citizens and businesses really matters and the leading role of the state in developing the comprehensive PR campaign is crucial. Therefore, it is important to engage journalists and realize the educational potential of the local media market, which could be regarded as one of the most active players in the society, since open data is a new idea and many people have not realized the political potential of the concept, which could change the fundamentals of governance by making it more transparent and accessible (see figure 5.2).

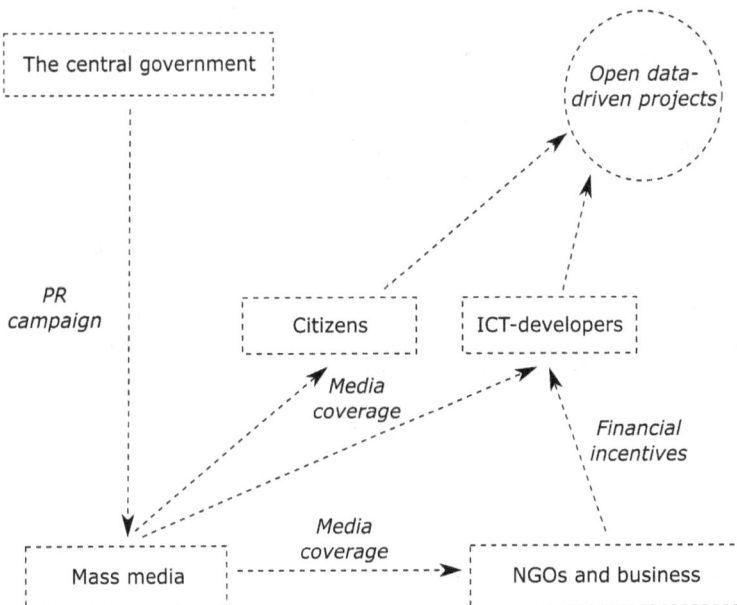

Figure 5.2 A potential media campaign that could help to generate public interest in the open data philosophy

Source: own illustration

The *principle of authenticity* is also an important aspect of the open data concept. In Kazakhstan, it is considered a part of information security in the system (The Open Government Project, 2015), since the authenticity of open data implies not only correctness of the government information but also its correspondence with existing regulation in the area. In this respect, not all documents according to the local laws could be published freely online, especially if they contain personal information or state or commercial secrets. Therefore, the statistical data are the most accepted type of data sets available on the portal. The typographical errors and incorrect formatting that happen sometimes, apparently due to time pressures and lack of technological readiness in public agencies, could be regarded as the most significant challenges in the operation of the open data concept at the technological level.

The *user friendliness* is, perhaps, one of the most controversial principles of the open data concept because practitioners and academics still suffer from limited understanding of what user friendliness is due to the complexity of the e-government systems and subjectivity of personal experiences. It is especially true for open data. They are all published in a machine-readable format and obviously are not ready for immediate use by citizens. The open data concept infers that the data sets should be first processed by third parties, who are usually ICT developers or technically savvy people but not the average citizens themselves. So, the user friendliness could only be related to the open data portal itself. In this regard, such technological features of the open data portal as the statistical tools that help to select open data in accordance with the popularity of the given government information, number of data sets, and information on its original source could be considered as the most important.

In general, all these five basic principles of open data can be regarded as the prerequisites of the open government concept aimed at establishing better communication between the state and its citizens. In this regard, it is necessary to distinguish the key target audiences that could presumably benefit the most from the implementation of the open data-driven projects, namely, citizens, nongovernmental organizations, ICT developers, businesses and public agencies.

Summary of the policy analysis: key findings and recommendations

In conclusion, the participation of citizens should be considered as the most important part of the open government concept since almost all data sets are related more or less to people and almost all PR campaigns of both state and nongovernmental organizations in this respect should be aimed at engaging citizens to the open data portal and, more important, *to the open data-driven platforms* created by the private sector and, in many cases, even by the citizens themselves. Therefore, the promotion of peer-to-peer collaboration should be an ultimate goal in Kazakhstan. The successful realization of the open data-driven projects could potentially enrich the political life of the country with new instruments to further political communication among citizens and eventually transform the traditional public mindset toward e-government and, in the end, democratic institutions of decision making by dramatically decentralizing them.

Indeed, all these projects demonstrate the development of the open government concept which is experiencing dramatic transformations in this post-Soviet nation, offering not only new opportunities to improve public administration and battle corruption, but also, what is more important, promoting new platforms to build a digital political culture where such aspects of modern democracy as civic engagement and civic participation could hopefully play a more important role in the further development of e-government and ICT-driven public sector reforms, of course, provided that it will be welcomed by the government leadership itself.

In this respect, it is necessary to distinguish three pillars of the new political culture that are presumably emerging in Kazakhstan due to the promotion of the open government projects, namely, e-government-driven civic engagement, collaboration and participation. Each one is somehow related to the development of the open lawmaking, open dialogue and open data project, respectively.

In conclusion, it is necessary to note that the policy makers and administrators of the open government projects should clearly understand that e-government is a multidimensional phenomenon that requires not only systematic support of the already launched public platforms but also an ability to see new perspective directions of its promotion, creating new political dimensions for the development of e-government and eventually e-democracy.

Today, Kazakhstan is arguably regarded by the United Nations as one of the most successful examples of ICT-driven reforms in public administration in Central and South Asia in its biennial ranking of the global e-government development among all emerging nations (UNPAN, 2014). One of the reasons of the success is not only due to the wealth of human and financial resources invested by the national authorities in the state-run e-government projects, which are aimed at achieving several crucial milestones in building digital government such as launching the single e-services portal, centralized databases and e-document management systems but, more important, due to a relentless desire of the national government to be noticed by the international community in this context (Åström et al., 2012). In fact, the implementation of e-government has become a matter of national priority in Kazakhstan where the image-making part – i.e. a notorious country PR (Marat, 2009) – is considered by policy makers as one of the most important components of the project, as a *sui generis* argument and a robust reference to arguably successful public reforms and even to a new emerging e-democracy in the international area.

So far, the PR strategy has been effective. All formal requirements in meeting certain benchmarks of a typical progressive e-government project, such as the launch of the special web portals and a number of e-services, were successfully implemented. Therefore, the country is steadily improving its stance in the global e-government rating list (UNPAN, 2010, 2012, 2014). However, the main challenge in realization of the entire concept has remained the same, which is how to effectively engage citizens in the e-government domain to successfully implement one of the most important parts of the concept – i.e. promoting *e-participation,* which is apparently becoming the number one feature in measuring the e-government's progress by the increasing number of global experts (Islam, 2008; Berntzen & Olsen, 2009; Rorissa, Demissie & Pardo, 2011; Bellio & Buccoliero, 2013; Fan & Luo, 2014). Moreover, the rapid diffusion of the open government concept worldwide as an exclusively political idea which is not only focused on building more effective public administration as a primary goal of the *traditional understanding of the e-government advancement* but also as a political movement aimed at making governments presumably more transparent and, most important, more collaborative.

In this regard, the collaboration implies the need to increase civic engagement – i.e. develop the weakest feature of e-government building in Kazakhstan when basically the good old methods of the concept promotion such as the ordinary top-down directives and direct generous funding do not work as effectively as before, since the political paradigm of e-government and society itself is transforming due to a changeable nature of information and communication technologies. The indirect pressure of the digital era on governments to reform is relentless, especially in societies that once embraced the social network-driven political communication. In this respect, the author of the book argues in Chapter 6 that the further realization of e-participation and civic engagement projects in Kazakhstan might be the most cost-effective answer to the challenges.

References

The Adilet Open Laws Project (2015). http://adilet.zan.kz/eng
Ak Orda (2007). *President Nursultan Nazarbayev Is Going to Hold an Internet-Conference on the 7th of June, 2007 and to Answer Questions of Users of the Global Network.* http://www.akorda.kz/pda.php/en/page/page_glava-gosudarstva-nursul tan-nazarbaev-7-iyunya-etogo-goda-provedet-internet-konf_1348723518

Åström, J., Karlsson, M., Linde, J., & Pirannejad, A. (2012). Understanding the rise of e-participation in non-democracies: Domestic and international factors. *Government Information Quarterly*, *29*(2), 142–150.

Bellio, E., & Buccoliero, L. (2013). Citizen web empowerment across Italian cities: A benchmarking approach. In C. Silva (Ed)., *Citizen E-Participation in Urban Governance: Crowdsourcing and Collaborative Creativity* (pp. 284–302). Hershey, PA: Information Science Reference.

Berntzen, L., & Olsen, M. G. (2009, February). Benchmarking e-government-a comparative review of three international benchmarking studies. In *Digital Society, 2009. ICDS'09. Third International Conference on* (pp. 77–82). New York: IEEE.

Bhuiyan, S. H. (2010). E-government in Kazakhstan: Challenges and its role to development. *Public Organization Review*, *10*(1), 31–47.

Bhuiyan, S. H. (2011). Trajectories of e-government implementation for public sector service delivery in Kazakhstan. *International Journal of Public Administration*, *34*(9), 604–615.

Bhuiyan, S. H. (2011b). Transition towards a knowledge-based society in post-communist Kazakhstan: Does good governance matter? *Journal of Asian and African Studies*, *46*(4), 404–421.

Bhuiyan, S. H., & Amagoh, F. (2011). Public sector reform in Kazakhstan: Issues and perspectives. *International Journal of Public Sector Management*, *24*(3), 227–249.

Davies, T. G., & Bawa, Z. A. (2012). The promises and perils of open government data (OGD). *The Journal of Community Informatics*, *8*(2). http://www.ci-journal.net/index.php/ciej/article/view/929/955

The Directive N 464 (2013, January 8). The State Program "Information Kazakhstan – 2020". http://adilet.zan.kz/rus/docs/U1300000464#z0

The E-Government Directive # 1471 (2004, November 10). The State Program of E-Government Formation in Kazakhstan for 2005–2007. The presidential directive. http://adilet.zan.kz/rus/docs/U040001471_

The E-Government of Kazakhstan (2015). www.egov.kz

Evans, A. M., & Campos, A. (2013). Open government initiatives: Challenges of citizen participation. *Journal of Policy Analysis and Management*, *32*(1), 172–185.

Fan, B., & Luo, J. (2014). Benchmarking scale of e-government stage in Chinese municipalities from government chief information officers' perspective. *Information Systems and e-Business Management*, *12*(2), 259–284.

Google Trends (2015). www.google.com/trends

The Internet-Conference Platform (2015). http://egov.kz/wps/portal/conference?lang=ru

Internews Kazakhstan (2015). http://www.internews.kz/

Islam, M. S. (2008). Towards a sustainable e-Participation implementation model. *European Journal of ePractice*, *5*(10), 1–12.

Janenova, S. (2010). E-Government in Kazakhstan: Challenges for a transitional country. In *18th NISPAcee Annual Conference "Public Administration in Times of Crisis"* (pp. 12–14). Warsaw, Poland.

Janssen, M., Charalabidis, Y., & Zuiderwijk, A. (2012). Benefits, adoption barriers and myths of open data and open government. *Information Systems Management*, *29*(4), 258–268.

Jäppinen, S., Toivonen, T., & Salonen, M. (2013). Modelling the potential effect of shared bicycles on public transport travel times in Greater Helsinki: An open data approach. *Applied Geography*, *43*, 13–24.

Johnson, E., & Kolko, B. (2010). e-Government and transparency in authoritarian regimes: Comparison of national-and city-level e-government web sites in Central Asia. *Digital Icons: Studies in Russian, Eurasian and Central European New Media*, *3*, 15–48.

Kassen, M. (2010). *E-Government in Kazakhstan: Realization and prospects*, 6. Carbondale: Open SIUC, Southern Illinois University. http://opensiuc.lib.siu.edu/pnconfs_2010/6/

Kassen, M. (2013). A promising phenomenon of open data: A case study of the Chicago open data project. *Government Information Quarterly*, *30*(4), 508–513.

Kassen, M. (2014). Globalization of e-government: Open government as a global agenda; benefits, limitations and ways forward. *Information Development*, *30*(1), 51–58.

Knox, C. (2008). Kazakhstan: Modernizing government in the context of political inertia. *International Review of Administrative Sciences*, *74*(3), 477–496.

Marat, E. (2009). Nation branding in Central Asia: A new campaign to present ideas about the state and the nation. *Europe-Asia Studies*, *61*(7), 1123–1136.

NITEC (2015). http://www.nitec.kz/index.php/en

Obama, B. (2009). Memorandum for the heads of executive departments and agencies. *Presidential Studies Quarterly*, *39*(3), 429.

The Official Blog-Platform in the Kostanay Region (2015). http://akim.blogs.kostanay.gov.kz

The Official Blog-Platform in the Pavlodar Region (2015). http://blog.pavlodar.gov.kz/

The Official Blog-Platform of Government Executives (2015). http://www.blogs.e.gov.kz/en

The Open Data Project (2013). http://data.egov.kz/

The Open Government Partnership (2015). http://www.opengovpartnership.org/

The Open Government Project (2015). http://open.egov.kz/

The Open Lawmaking Platform (2015). http://legalacts.egov.kz/

Reuters (2007). Kazakhs Shower President with Cryptic Questions. http://www.reuters.com/article/2007/06/01/us-kazakhstan-webcast-idUSL0131903220070601

Rorissa, A., Demissie, D., & Pardo, T. (2011). Benchmarking e-government: A comparison of frameworks for computing e-government index and ranking. *Government Information Quarterly*, *28*(3), 354–362.

Schwegmann, C. (2013). Open data in developing countries. *European Public Sector Information Platform Topic Report*, (2013/02).

Soros Foundation (2015). www.ru.soros.kz

UNPAN (2010). The Global E-Government Survey. Leveraging E-government at a Time of Financial and Economic Crisis. http://www2.unpan.org/egovkb/global_reports/10report.htm

UNPAN (2012). The Global E-Government Survey. E-Government for the People. http://unpan3.un.org/egovkb/Portals/egovkb/Documents/un/2012-Survey/unpan048065.pdf

UNPAN (2014). The Global E-Government Survey. E-Government for the Future We Want. http://unpan3.un.org/egovkb/Reports/UN-E-Government-Survey-2014

Verheijen, T. (2007). Public administration in post-communist states. In B. G. Peters & J. Pierre (Eds.), *Handbook of public administration* (pp. 311–319). London: SAGE Publications Ltd.

Wang, X., & Wan Wart, M. (2007). When public participation in administration leads to trust: An empirical assessment of managers' perceptions. *Public Administration Review, 67*(2), 265–278.

6 E-participation and civic engagement in Kazakhstan

A political or technological dimension of e-government?

Kazakhstan might be regarded today as a poster child of the global e-government movement and promising opportunities that related e-participation platforms could offer in the realization of major public administration projects in a typical developing and transitional society. Especially, it is true in highlighting the potential contribution of the interactive technologies to enhance public sector reforms and renovate bureaucratic and cumbersome public service delivery systems, which many post-Soviet and post-totalitarian nations in transition have been notoriously famous for, including Kazakhstan. In this regard, various international e-government surveys carried out by the panel of experts from the United Nations and World Bank argue that this nation has generally succeeded in transforming its public sector institutions by resorting to various digital collaborative and participatory platforms, especially at the national level. In this respect, this chapter will analyze the true political and socioeconomic incentives that lie behind the mere desire of the national authorities to improve public administration in Kazakhstan through the adoption of various e-participation strategies and concepts, focusing, especially, on studying the related activity of wiki-based, open data-driven and social media projects, locating current and prospective drivers and barriers in introducing a new philosophy of civic engagement and proactive political participation, providing some generalizations on promising aspects of using other e-government innovations and offering ways forward for both academics and practitioners on how to overcome the challenges.

Building a framework for policy analysis

The purpose of policy analysis

The primary purpose of the research is to investigate the promising potential of the e-participation platforms to advance public sector innovations in

Kazakhstan and trace the emergence of the related culture of civic engagement and public collaboration to understand how the phenomena affect the democratization of political communication processes in an unusual context of a typical developing and post-totalitarian country.

The methodological framework

This case study research, which begins with the context analysis of the key driving forces in the e-participation movement such as the investigation of the global, political and socioeconomic incentives that would help to explain the true motives of the national authorities to promote various digital participatory and collaborative projects in Kazakhstan and generate new hypotheses and arguments. Another dimension of the research is the policy analysis of the key realization strategies and tools embraced by policy makers in the e-government sphere, such as the widespread policy of e-centralism – i.e. total executive control of the national government and single public funding in the realization of all ICT-driven public sector reforms, as well as a primary focus on the nationwide multidimensional informatization strategies. One of the most important parts of the case study is the content analysis of the six key e-participation projects that could help to draw a detailed picture of the interesting technological dimension of the e-participation movement in Kazakhstan and test the previous hypothesis and generate new assumptions. Finally, the author of the research turns his attention to the analysis of the fundamental barriers that policy makers face in the diffusion of the e-participation philosophy among other stakeholders and offers several recommendations on how to overcome the challenges.

The key drivers of the e-participation movement in Kazakhstan

The global incentives: globalization of e-government technologies

In Kazakhstan, one of the key drivers in the realization of not only e-participation platforms but also the e-government concept as a whole is a global trend in the diffusion of various digital public sector projects worldwide (West, 2007). In fact, the ICT-driven public administration is universally regarded as a logical continuation of the promising idea to use new information technologies in the e-commerce sector, relying on solutions that were originally developed in the corporate sphere (e.g. in various e-procurement and online trade systems) and only later adopted for public purposes by governments in many countries (Moon, 2002; Tat Kei Ho,

2002; Carter & Bélanger, 2005). As a typical transitional state, Kazakhstan often tries to copy and adopt the best practices from all over the world in reforming various spheres of economy, including in the e-commerce and e-government areas. Moreover, taking into account the increasing popularity of the open government and open data movements worldwide, the related concept of e-democracy is experiencing a fundamental shift in its understanding as a certain hallmark of the digital revolution in a political context. In this regard, government authorities are beginning to realize the value of participatory and collaborative solutions in the e-government sphere, which could be used to globally demonstrate a formal promotion of civic engagement through sophisticated e-participation platforms and systems. The United Nations and its multiple institutions play a crucial role in the indirect diffusion of the conceptual platforms thanks to the organization of various international competitions and cross-country comparative researches and surveys in the area that closely monitor the development of e-participation worldwide in all its diversity as a multidimensional phenomenon, commenting and grading any achievements and progress in the sphere by the member states, regardless of whether they are developing or emerging economies. As a result, this rapid and widespread globalization of various participatory platforms all over the world became an important indicator of the national political and socioeconomic development and any achievement and progress in the sphere could be measured and graded accordingly at the global level, causing an unofficial competition among countries and regions as well as allowing new qualification benchmarks and goals, even if they often remain a mere formality.

The political incentives: the promise of direct digital democracy or global country PR?

The development of various participatory and collaborative platforms is regarded as one of the most promising ways to further not only governance in its classic, almost ancient, form of direct democracy but also to improve traditional perceptions of state, transforming it as a collaborative and open enterprise that should be based on principles of accountability and transparency. The active use of various e-democracy solutions such as wiki-based, open data and social media-driven platforms in promoting civic engagement and e-participation in an attempt to make the public sector reforms less costly due to the phenomena of crowdsourcing and collective brainstorming as well as the recent trend in the diffusion of the open data strategies in many developed nations that conceptually rely on the participation of citizens in the creation of related independent open data-driven projects and interactive e-government startups might harbinger a new era in enhancing the traditional public administration systems, especially in transitional and post-totalitarian societies, with promising new ways to democratize the established channels of political communication, making them proactive as never before due to the use of peer-to-peer civic engagement platforms. Thus, any developments in this direction are generally associated in the academic and professional literature with progress in furthering democracy itself (Cegarra-Navarro, Pachón & Cegarra, 2012; Linders, 2012). In addition, the launch of various international ranking lists of the most developed countries in terms of e-government development, including in the sphere of e-participation, allows Kazakhstan to ostensibly demonstrate some progress in building participatory democracy by resorting paradoxically only to the public sector reforms and skipping any political transformations, leaving intact the key aspects of the post-totalitarian political and economic system. This measure could potentially improve the international image and global stance of the country as an emerging digital democracy in various global contests and rankings, at least, formally. It is especially important in the light of the upcoming world exhibition Expo 2017 in Astana that will be convened in 2017 and the overall extreme desire of national authorities to pose globally the country as a technologically advanced state.

The economic incentives: prospects to further the national economy and battle corruption

One of the main economic incentives to implement the e-participation platforms in Kazakhstan lies in a pragmatic goal of the central government to harness the promising potential of ICT to save large financial resources that the national authorities usually spend annually on various public sector projects, which are usually aimed at not only fighting red tape but also improving the business environment in the country. It is especially important in funding any public sector reforms to take into account the existing unitary structure of the public administration system and highly centralized system of budget allocations. In this regard, the use of crowdsourcing and independent collaborative tools and, more important, the convergence of the related e-participation projects with various e-government and e-procurement platforms, presumably could help the public agencies to understand better the needs of citizens and businesses as well as ensure the creation of new channels of communication and collaboration with people to battle corruption and rampant red tape, which are still regarded as the most notorious barriers in the successful transformation of the country as a developed nation, and furthermore, find better solutions to improve governance at the local level by resorting to a promising phenomenon of civic engagement and collective decision making in the sphere.

The social incentives: creating new social network channels

In Kazakhstan, civic engagement and e-participation can also be regarded as additional tools to improve public relations with government at both national and local levels and to ensure interactive feedback from citizenry on various issues to ease potential social tensions and conflicts in the future, which appear to become more likely in societies in transition and in countries that have not managed to react properly to indirect bottom-up signals in a dramatic environment of ongoing financial instability in the world, especially in societies that rely heavily on an unsustainable raw material-based economy. Moreover, the online presence of government and use of social media by public figures and politicians is crucial to ensure the successful feedback with potential constituents (Bertot, Jaeger & Grimes, 2010; Castells, 2015) and, in general, could be useful in boosting the image of government both internationally and domestically. This reason is why so many politicians in Kazakhstan resort to social networks not only as a powerful tool in developing new channels of political communication with peers and other colleagues but also as an instrument to maintain and improve a media image as ostensibly transparent and open-minded leaders in a more convenient and cost-efficient manner.

The key realization tools of the e-participation reforms

E-centralism as an ubiquitous strategy of the movement

In Kazakhstan, the nation is built on the principle of a top-down structure of power relations and unambiguous electronic centralism or e-centralism in public administration and political institutions at all levels of governance that discourages any autonomy of public opinion and strong opposition. One of the most important prerequisites in the realization of the ICT-driven public sector reforms is a strong political will of the national authorities to succeed in building an effective e-government and to be on par, at least formally, with the most developed nations in the world. Traditionally, all public sector reforms are fully realized and successfully implemented at the local level only if there are strong political signals and, most important, strict organizational control and administrative pressure exerted by the centralized government agencies at various institutional levels. In this respect, the political support of the central government and individual commitments taken by the heads of various public agencies is crucial in advancing the e-participation platforms, especially at different institutional levels, taking into account the multidimensional nature of the e-government phenomenon.

In addition, this strictly centralized realization strategy should also provide a favorable playground to promote promising concepts such as e-democracy and open government. Furthermore, the obvious political trend in supporting and furthering the potential of platforms such as civic engagement and e-participation as effective political instruments to improve the standing and international reputation of the country in various e-government ratings and opportunities to import new technologies of social control feed a relentless desire of the central government to implement the projects in Kazakhstan. Consequently, the implementation of all projects related to the e-government area is, to a greater extent, regarded as a strategy of national priority and all other factors, such as proper financing and associated legal regulation of the e-participation sphere, could be directly associated with a strong political will to support e-government projects as a whole, since the national government puts up money and helps to unexceptionally materialize them all.

Direct funding of all ICT-driven public sector projects

The next powerful instrument in the realization of e-participation projects in Kazakhstan is systematic and generous funding of the major ICT-driven public reforms from the national budget. Since the development of e-government, and more generally, the informatization of the public sector is regarded as part of much wider state-sponsored programs such as the industrialization of the local economy and technological advancement of the nation, covering almost all aspects of socioeconomic life, the financial support of the related projects has been increasingly provided by the central government in recent years. As a result, the political will and financial capability of the nation to fund the public sector initiatives have opened incredible opportunities to realize ambitious ICT-driven public sector reforms, unmatched by its scale in the modern history of the country, boosting the national e-government readiness and potentially paving the way to introduce the participatory and collaborative components of the concept. Moreover, further commitments of the government to finance future projects in the sphere create a promising playground to implement civic engagement and e-participation platforms, transforming not only the traditional system of public administration – that is, the initial goal of the e-government concept in Kazakhstan – but also changing the nature of public sector reforms, harnessing both political and economic benefits of the e-participation phenomenon in boosting the international image of government itself and, less important, outsourcing some of the government services (see figure 6.1).

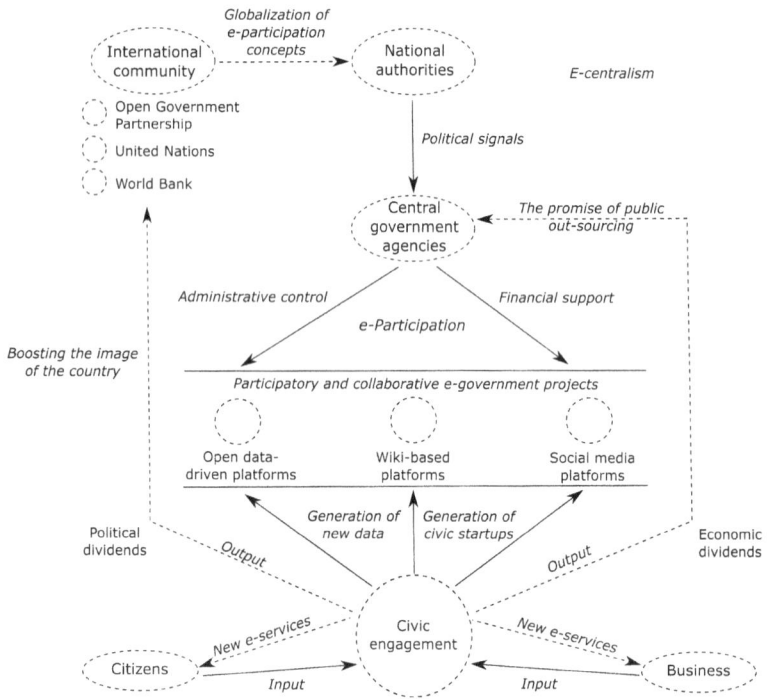

Figure 6.1 A potentially sustainable way to realize the e-participation platforms in Kazakhstan through e-centralism (hypothesis)

Source: own illustration

The focus on nationwide multidimensional informatization strategies

The third instrument in the realization of civic engagement and participatory initiatives is the harmonization of the e-government programs with corresponding nationwide informatization strategies at all levels of government. Most important, the implementation of the official e-government projects was conceptualized in several strategic documents issued in 2004 (The e-Government Directive # 1471, 2004) and 2007 (The Government Resolution N 1155–1, 2007) that provided a robust legal platform to further many ideas and initiatives in this sphere. Another strategy that generally regulates the adoption of the e-participatory platforms is the strategy "Information Kazakhstan 2020" (The Directive N 464, 2013) and The Freedom of Information Act (2015), which intrinsically focus the attention of government agencies on the realization of various collaborative platforms in the e-government area, especially of those that relate to the operation of the open data-driven projects and social media startups. Furthermore, these documents explicitly aim to achieve certain progress in increasing the ranking of the country in various ICT rating lists, including in the e-participation sphere, such as entering the panel of the most advanced nations in the world in terms of e-government development. All these documents send a strong political signal for both national and local government agencies to concentrate all of their resources on the realization of the e-participation projects. In this regard, it is interesting to note that any promotion of the national e-government platforms in the global ratings, especially in those that are administered by the United Nations and World Bank, is regarded as a direct indication of progress.

The realization of the e-participation projects: is it just a fancy media entourage?

One of the interesting aspects in the implementation of the e-participation concept in Kazakhstan is the active realization of the official interactive projects designed for both citizens and businesses by the central government, regardless of whether they are promoted at the national or local levels. For example, various Internet conferences, public discussions, e-mail communication with public servants, online appointments to the ministers, blog platforms of the chief executives, the contacts of people with officials in social media and direct participation in the development of the open data-driven projects are among the most promising platforms that allow citizens of Kazakhstan to participate in digital communication with government, using the principle of the single centralized registration that is available on all official e-government platforms.

The promise of social media-driven political communication in Kazakhstan

Social media is one of the most promising platforms harnessed today in Kazakhstan, indirectly changing the traditional channels of political communication, at least in the eyes of mass media. The social networks-driven communication is beginning to play, in this regard, an ever-increasing role in the public sphere (The Officials in Social Networks Project, 2014), affecting both the executive and legislative branches of power. The institutional and personal accounts of the chief directors in the central and local government agencies, as well as members of the national parliament in various social media, help them to communicate with other stakeholders of the e-government movement: journalists, administrators, lobby groups from the business sector and, less often, their own constituents at the regions in an attempt to be like other peers, and what is more important, like the highest political figures. In fact, the so-called boom of the social media revolution in Kazakhstan could be traced back to the first attempts by Kazakh Prime Minister Karim Massimov to introduce the public value of Facebook and Twitter applications to members of his cabinet as early as 2009. He was the first senior politician to realize the power of social networks and actively began to use this new channel of communication with people. From that moment on, almost every top and even middle-level civil servant has been expected to open a wide range of personal accounts in English, Russian or Kazakh social media platforms and actively use them in everyday communication with media and citizens, even if in many cases it was just a formality. The popularity of the social network-driven communication, related public agiotage and even some journalistic entourage around it has transformed the media image of e-government in Kazakhstan and opened new opportunities not only for public figures but also for technically savvy citizens to be heard, at least in social media and other related channels of communication. In this regard, among the most often used social networks platforms are Facebook, Twitter, Mail.ru, Vkontakte, On.kz, YouTube and Kaztube (The Internet Statistics of Kazakhstan, 2015). In general, the global and Russian-based social media platforms are much more popular among government officials in Kazakhstan than domestic ones.

The Internet-conference platform: a tool of public relations or internal institutional and bureaucratic control?

The Internet conference project allows citizens and legal residents of Kazakhstan to put online their questions and petitions to *akims* (i.e. governors or mayors in Kazakh) of various regions and cities (The Internet-Conference Platform, 2014). Perhaps, it is one of the most promising e-participation initiatives launched recently at the national level, since it allows petitioners to build effective channels of communication with the heads of local governments. It appears to be especially useful in a unitary state such as Kazakhstan where people often apply to the central government, which often means to physically go to the capital city of Astana, to solve their problems at the local level. In this regard, the development of the project could help to popularize the public value of the participatory and collaborative nature of e-government at the regional level. Taking into account the size of the country and lack of good roads, the development of the Internet-conference platform could result in better inclusion of the local population in regional affairs and, more important, help to promote greater accountability of the governors before the central government, since, although the majority of the online conferences are organized with the participation of local akims, the platform itself is realized and, most important, monitored at the national level, using the unified authorization procedures and single government databases, providing the central public agencies with a strong instrument of administrative control over the regional authorities. In this regard, the open media transmission of the online conference sessions allows the national and local journalistic communities to cover the entire administrative procedure and analyze the most important public issues and topics, collective or individual petitions and administrative decisions, providing an additional instrument of public scrutiny in the sphere.

The Public Discussion Platform: crowdsourcing new e-government ideas

The public discussion initiative is one of the most promising projects that might change the nature of decision making in the realization of e-government concepts in Kazakhstan by transforming the traditional communication channels of government information and providing great opportunities for citizens and businesses to express their own opinions and even indirectly participate in the reformation of the existing e-service delivery concepts, generating new e-government ideas and recommendations. The main principle of the project is to provide a participatory platform that would help to brainstorm and discuss various concepts on how to reform the public sector in all its diversity as well as analyze the content in the draft versions of legislative bills and state programs before their adoption by parliament and official publication (The Public Discussion Platform, 2014). One of the interesting aspects of the project is that technologically it is embedded in the existing paradigm of the single e-government system, which helps to simplify the registration and administration of the personal accounts of citizens in other e-participation platforms, allowing it to smoothly operate with all related transactions in an interactive mode, regardless of whether citizens are accessing them from the desktop computers or mobile applications. In this regard, the widespread use of mobile operating systems, such as the Apple iOS and Android, can help this participatory platform to potentially increase the number of registered users in the e-government system as a whole. Moreover, taking into account the popularity of social media networks and mobile technologies in Kazakhstan, the diversification of registration methods in these platforms could help the government to maintain an almost ideal around-the-clock interactive contact line with all citizens, providing a great opportunity, for example, to send alerts, organize various online polls, survey and market research, potentially receiving useful feedback from millions of users, who are currently registered in the entire system of e-government. It also provides a promising communication platform to popularize interactively various e-services, including those that are related to the e-participation paradigm.

The Electronic Address Platform: tracking the civic applications and queries

This e-participation project helps people to track interactively the status of their messages, application and official letters to various government agencies (The Electronic Address Platform, 2014). Most important, citizens have the option to receive a guarantee that their applications will be delivered on time to the right person and receive a reaction or response from the corresponding agencies, providing a powerful instrument for members of the civil society to be in online contact with the government. The main idea of the e-participation platform is to provide people with personalized electronic services that help them to track all documents and transactions online, using a universal unique authorization number in the system, which again simplifies administration of the project. Taking into account the existence of the single e-government platform, operating on the whole territory of Kazakhstan as well as the use of nationwide identification numbers and single databases of government information, regardless of whether they are accessed at the national or local levels of governance, the Electronic Address Platform can boost all related administrative procedures, fighting the traditional rampant culture of red tape and bureaucracy in many public agencies. The existing laws implicitly require the government agencies to answer civic petitions, applications and queries within a certain period of time, which range from a few days to several weeks, guaranteeing, to some extent, a proper reaction from public servants and providing an effective instrument of administrative control, internal executive assessment of management and formalization of career promotion in public administration.

Open data in Kazakhstan: raw material for e-participation platforms or why the publication of government data sets is not enough?

Officially, the main political idea of the national data portal was to promote transparency of the public sector and boost the development of new channels of political communication between government institutions and citizens (The Open Data Project, 2013). The project was presumably designed to provide citizens with free access to various data sets derived from an extremely wide range of government agencies. In this regard, conceptually, open data can be regarded as a type of raw material in building independent e-participation projects that would help various ICT developers and technically savvy citizens to produce their own open data-driven applications and hybrid computer programs such as mashups, wiki-based and social media solutions, using a massive amount of government data, statistical records, national archival files, geostationary and geographic data, official contact information and various nationwide semiofficial registries, etc. However, despite the fact that the project, which has already published more than seven hundred data sets (The E-Government of Kazakhstan, 2015), could potentially change the nature of government-citizen communication and e-participation in this country, there is a shortage of independent open data-driven startups and initiatives.

Theoretically, the open data concept can be regarded as one of the most prospective ways to further civic engagement in Kazakhstan in a completely innovative manner, provided that its adoption will be accompanied with the promotion of new politically collaborative realization strategies and tactics. In this regard, it is important to enhance public awareness in the e-participation sphere, resorting to the promise of public outreach and public relations campaigns in mass media and social networks. It becomes clear that the launch of official participatory platforms and publication of government data sets will not guarantee a higher level of civic engagement in the sphere. In order to close this fundamental conceptual gap between public and civic components of the open data realization policies, the phenomenon, which could be tentatively called *a great e-participation division* (see figure 6.2), it is crucial to apply more sophisticated strategies in popularizing the new philosophy of open government and e-participation among ICT developers and technically savvy citizens and, most important, embrace more collaborative approaches in promoting civic engagement in the political arena, the fundamental principles of freedom of information and opinions in mass media and social networks. After all, without cardinal changes in the political culture and public mindset of the post-totalitarian society, it would be extremely difficult to achieve tangible results in building true digital democracy in Kazakhstan and the ostensibly progressive accomplishments in the e-government sphere will remain an expensive fancy adornment in a completely inert and paradoxically different political environment, an ironic testament of unfulfilled promises.

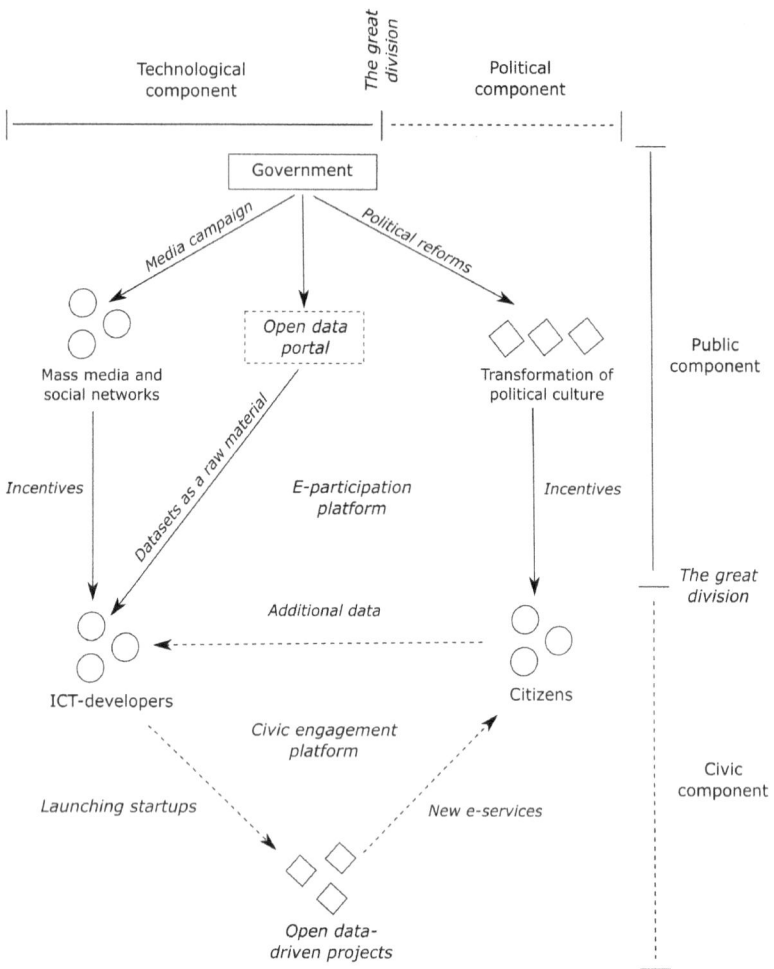

Figure 6.2 The great e-participation division between the public and civic components in the development of the open data-driven realization philosophy (hypothesis)

Source: own illustration

The fundamental challenges of the e-participation movement in Kazakhstan: key findings

The perils of e-bureaucracy or the emergence of a new type of red tape

Ironically, the paradox of the ICT-driven public sector reforms in Kazakhstan is that the top-down and one-way mechanism of its realization, which is popular among policy makers in advancing e-government, appears to be ineffective in promoting the civic component in the e-participation platforms. The key challenge is how to engage citizens. In fact, nearly all national e-government projects are initiated, funded and implemented by the government through directives and traditional administrative commands without any participation of the private sector. In this respect, one of the most important ingredients of the e-participation philosophy, especially when resorting to the multidimensional phenomenon of open data – i.e. civic engagement and indirect involvement of the nongovernmental sector – is often significantly underestimated in the final equations of the open government realization policies. Even though the ICT-driven public sector reforms and related e-government innovations help reduce the public spending and battle corruption, the fundamentals of traditional governance remain the same – i.e. the bureaucratic barriers and mindset of the post-totalitarian society are the most difficult to change due to the inertia in public mentality. Although the trend is slowly changing, the widespread slogan that economy is a number one priority is still relevant in any reforms, especially in relationship to the system transformation of political values. In this regard, even the obvious advancement of the official e-participation platforms due to the emergence of new interactive and collaborative tools is more a byproduct of the relentless e-government implementation tactics aimed at boosting global media image rather than an ultimate goal of the realization policy.

The inertia of public mentality and illusive prospects for civic engagement

Kazakhstan is still a country in transition where many political ideas such as civic engagement or citizen participation are new and could not be realized only by the individual members of the civil society without the overall transformation of political culture and, therefore, it would be naive to presume that e-participation platforms alone could quickly change the bureaucratic nature of public administration and further digital democracy. Perhaps, this is one of the reasons why governments all over the world are slowly beginning to make tentative attempts to resort to the principle of crowd-sourcing in launching various interactive and collaborative e-services, for instance, in promoting open data contests and wiki-based platforms or inviting citizens to participate in various online surveys in official web portals. After all, e-government, in general, and e-participation, in particular, is just a technological platform, which for its full inclusion into the ideological realm of the open government philosophy requires social interactivity and active engagement of the key stakeholders – i.e. citizens, developers and independent ICT experts, nongovernmental organizations and mass media – to the e-government movement and, most important, the embracing of crucial factors such as the widespread culture of independent and critical thinking, a proactive stance of the civil society in the decision-making processes and new dynamic channels of political dialogue.

The lack of regulation and collaborative political culture in the e-participation sphere

In Kazakhstan, the theoretical possibility to harness the promising phenomenon of civic engagement, the results of which presumably could be used in the decision-making processes related to the introduction of participatory and open government political culture, especially concerning the promotion of wiki-based and open data-driven projects, is not properly accompanied by the corresponding harmonization of the innovations with the key provisions of the existing e-government regulatory acts. These laws usually regulate a limited area of the ICT-driven public sector reforms. In this respect, although there are several good legal instruments in the public administration sphere, which were mentioned earlier in the book, the implementation of the government-initiated platforms explicitly continues to be a number one priority, in general, with all controversial realization policies intact, such as the widespread use of traditional directives, top-down administrative commands and direct funding from the national budget. In fact, such new ideas as the promotion of open data, use of civic engagement and participation tools in the e-government area are not reflected in the existing legislation. The fundamental challenge, in this respect, is related to the aptitude of the corresponding political and regulatory institutions to quickly adapt the long-established and well-developed e-government strategies such as super e-centralism and transactional e-service platforms, which proved to be effective in the conditions of the unitary public administration system in Kazakhstan, to the ever-changing nature of the e-participation phenomenon, which is currently experiencing a fundamental shift from a tool of public sector reforms toward a more collaborative and participatory political paradigm.

Summary of the analysis

The development of the e-participation movement in Kazakhstan is an interesting phenomenon to study, since it allows us not only to observe and analyze in detail the realization of such presumably universal and modern tool of public sector reforms as e-government in a typical emerging and transitional country but also to better understand a potentially promising role of the civic engagement projects to dramatically change the nature of the ICT-driven political communication in a post-totalitarian society. By resorting to the new collaborative technologies such as wiki-based, social media and open data-driven platforms, which had been originally aimed at furthering its sophisticated e-participation systems, Kazakhstan faced a number of fundamental challenges that, along with ongoing public sector reforms, also would require the transformation of the old public administration system that it inherited from its Soviet totalitarian past. In this respect, it is necessary to note that despite significant investments and strategic efforts to promote infrastructural and technological readiness of the national economy, which have created favorable conditions to promote ICT-driven public sector reforms and dramatically advance the e-participation platforms, the further development of the institution will require a fundamental ideological shift in public mindset and widespread adoption of the civic engagement philosophy by all stakeholders of the e-government movement.

References

Bertot, J. C., Jaeger, P. T., & Grimes, J. M. (2010). Using ICTs to create a culture of transparency: E-government and social media as openness and anti-corruption tools for societies. *Government Information Quarterly*, *27*(3), 264–271.

Carter, L., & Bélanger, F. (2005). The utilization of e-government services: Citizen trust, innovation and acceptance factors. *Information Systems Journal*, *15*(1), 5–25.

Castells, M. (2015). *Networks of outrage and hope: Social movements in the Internet age*. Hoboken: John Wiley & Sons.

Cegarra-Navarro, J. G., Pachón, J. R. C., & Cegarra, J. L. M. (2012). E-government and citizen's engagement with local affairs through e-websites: The case of Spanish municipalities. *International Journal of Information Management*, *32*(5), 469–478.

The Directive N 464 (2013, January 8). The State Program "Information Kazakhstan – 2020". http://adilet.zan.kz/rus/docs/U1300000464#z0

The E-Government Directive # 1471 (2004, November 10). The State Program of E-Government Formation in Kazakhstan for 2005–2007. The presidential directive. http://adilet.zan.kz/rus/docs/U040001471_

The E-Government of Kazakhstan (2015). www.egov.kz

The Electronic Address Platform (2014). http://egov.kz/wps/portal/citizensGovernment

The Freedom of Information Act (2015, November 16). The Kazakh Law on Access to Information. Law # 401-V (2015). http://online.zakon.kz/Document/? doc_id=39415981

The Government Resolution N 1155–1 (2007, November 30). The Program of E-Government Formation in Kazakhstan for 2008–2010. http://adilet.zan.kz/rus/ docs/P0700011551

The Internet-Conference Platform (2014). http://egov.kz/wps/portal/conference

The Internet Statistics of Kazakhstan (2015). www.zero.kz

Linders, D. (2012). From e-government to we-government: Defining a typology for citizen coproduction in the age of social media. *Government Information Quarterly*, *29*(4), 446–454.

Moon, M. J. (2002). The evolution of e-government among municipalities: Rhetoric or reality?. *Public Administration Review*, *62*(4), 424–433.

The Officials in Social Networks Project (2014). http://egov.kz/wps/portal/Content? contentPath=/egovcontent/citizensgovernment/articlesforcg/passport/off_twi &lang=en

The Open Data Project (2013). http://data.egov.kz

The Public Discussion Platform (2014). http://egov.kz/wps/portal/ContentDiscussion

Tat Kei Ho, A. (2002). Reinventing local governments and the e-government initiative. *Public Administration Review*, *62*(4), 434–444.

West, D. (2007). Global e-government, 2007. http://www.insidepolitics.org/egovt07 int.pdf

7   Key drivers, stakeholders and challenges of the e-government movement in Kazakhstan

Recommendations for practitioners

This chapter presents generalizations on the key findings of the case study with a primary focus on further discussion of the main assumptions presented in previous chapters of the research. In particular, the author tried to analyze the most important political, economic and social drivers; identify the key policy makers of the e-government movement in Kazakhstan in the public, nongovernmental and private sectors of the national economy and its main issues; highlight fundamental challenges such as a lack of internal institutional competition among its stakeholders, absence of constructive political opposition in the sphere, no participation of the business sector, local universities and think tanks in developing the concept, etc. In addition, some policy recommendations are proposed that the e-government practitioners and entrepreneurs could find useful in improving the operation of various digital public sector platforms and projects. Although e-government has traditionally been regarded both in academic and professional literature as a modern tool in reforming public administration, it is also beginning to play an important role as a universal theoretical paradigm and sometimes even a platform that encompasses and integrates all ICT-driven public sector transformations in all its diversity in one physical venue. In this regard, the case study of Kazakhstan clearly demonstrates that e-government should be regarded as a multidimensional phenomenon, taking into account not only various political, socioeconomic, geographical and administrative aspects of the country contexts that apparently have direct implications on its development but also such indirect domains of the concept promotion as foreign policy and mass media, making the traditional scientific trend that usually focuses on investigating only public administration-related projects too narrow and lopsided without inclusion in the analysis of all dimensions of the phenomenon.

Key drivers, strategies and realization tools of the e-government movement

Political drivers: boosting domestic and global public relations

One of the main political drivers that motivates national authorities to promote e-government is the realization of all ICT-driven public sector projects in Kazakhstan, including in the e-government sphere, is regarded by
the political leadership of the country as a matter of national priority. In
fact, e-government is widely considered in many regulatory, strategic and
executive documents as well as in public speeches and social media con-
versations of top politicians and prominent public figures as a technological
platform that could help the nation not only to boost economic development, especially in improving its obsolete and ineffective public administration system inherited from the post-Soviet past and even increasing political
communication with citizens, but also promote the image of the country
in the international arena (Stier, 2015) by raising the overall stance of the
national e-government project in various global ratings. In this regard, the
project itself is aimed at achieving two main objectives in maintaining good
public relations with people, since the realization of the e-government platforms will be widely supported as a tool that presumably makes the lives
of citizens easier due to the automation of many public administration processes and provision of interactive e-services, and second, in increasing
the international political image of the country as a modern and technologically advanced nation, since, of all innovation-driven public platforms
that were aimed at the fundamental transformation of the national economy,
e-government is probably the only area where it has been possible to achieve
impressive results in a short time period. In this connection, paradoxically,
the traditional top-down mechanism of decision making and administrative
control that was usually utilized in realizing various strategic programs and
reflected in the adoption of various executive directives has proven to be
successful in promoting e-government, despite the arguable collaborative
nature of the phenomenon itself that presumably requires civic engagement
and increased levels of e-participation. In addition, the centralized unitary
structure of public administration and governance in Kazakhstan with direct
and unambiguous pyramidal control of the administrative center in regions
makes this bureaucratic instrument much more effective and even results in
the adoption of e-government policies that are impossible to implement in
federal and many semi-unitary nations. In fact, e-centralism (Kassen, 2015),
in contrast to e-federalism in the United States and *a fortiori* e-confederalism
in the European Union, respectively, should be regarded as a large political

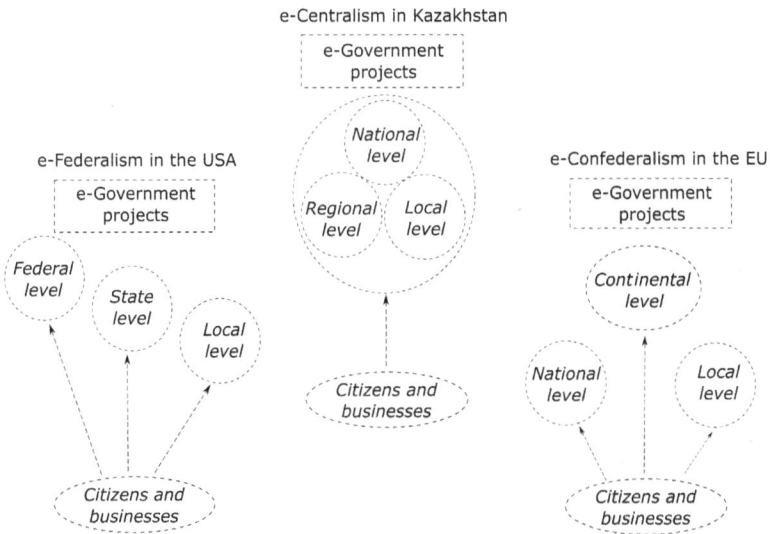

Figure 7.1 The political and organizational advantage of e-centralism in Kazakhstan
Source: own illustration

advantage of the e-government project in Kazakhstan (see figure 7.1) that helps this typical unitary state to advance the concept more effectively, resorting to a less collaborative participative yet practical and much speedier approach with distinctive features of its realization such as single databases, centralized authorization, one operator and processing center, a crucial role of the centralized budget funding and administrative control, etc.

Key political drivers:

- Improving the administrative coordination among government agencies
- Activating public relations and political communication with citizens
- Boosting global political and technological image of the country

Key realization strategies:

- Top-down mechanisms of administrative control
- Single realization strategy and tactics
- Focus on the most effective e-government projects

Key realization platforms:

- Open government project
- Open data project
- Open lawmaking project

Economic drivers: optimizing public administration systems

The universally accepted account that e-government could presumably be a great tool to improve and optimize the operation of the public administration systems is one of the main economic incentives to implement the concept in Kazakhstan. The introduction and development of various one-stop shop centers all over the country, which should be regarded as an intrinsic part of the national e-government platform, the launch of the single e-government portal that provides various interactive and transactional services to citizens and businesses, the publication of public information and data sets in machine-readable formats within the open data program, etc. – they are all presumably aimed at making the work of the public sector more effective and less costly for the state budget, especially under the current economic situation when this nation is experiencing fundamental financial challenges with serious shortages in the recharge of public funds that traditionally fueled the development of many ICT-driven projects. The unprecedented low prices for raw materials in the global commodity markets, especially for oil and non-ferrous metals, severely questioned the sustainability of the current lopsided model of economic development (Husain et al., 2015), in which Kazakhstan depends too much on revenues from the sale of natural resources. In this regard, the ICT-driven public sector projects such as national e-procurement and e-commerce initiatives, e-voting and, of course, e-government could provide public agencies with new cost-effective solutions in public administration on how to save significant financial resources due to the dividends that they could receive from a less-corrupt public service and more transparent public procurements.

Another important driver of the e-government movement is the opportunity to establish new digital channels for better communication with the business sector within the realization of several digital projects aimed at providing various information and transactional services. The launch of ICT-driven initiatives and startups under a single e-government platform such as e-licensing, e-business (Damu, 2015), e-payment, e-notary and many other interactive projects, the most prominent of which were analyzed in previous chapters of the book, provides not only various public services for local entrepreneurs but also is apparently intended to improve the business reputation of the country among potential foreign investors, taking into account that many projects provide their e-services in English for non-residents. In this regard, this *sui generis* digital PR strategy partly proved to be effective, since Kazakhstan managed to dramatically improve its ranking in a highly regarded and trustworthy rating list such as "The Ease of Doing Business," administered by the World Bank, which was reflected in its latest report (The World Bank, 2016), highlighting significant progress in the sphere due to the launch of more expedited services and initiatives.

Key economic drivers:

• Optimizing the operation of public administration
• Increasing transparency of public procurement
• Ensuring better communication with businesses and investors

Key realization strategies:

• Introduction of various interactive and transactional services
• Systematic publication of government information and data sets
• Special e-government projects for businesses and investors

Key realization platforms:

• E-Licensing Project
• E-Payment Project
• E-Notary Project

Social drivers: maintaining social stability

The development of various e-government projects, which for the last decade have dramatically changed the lives of average citizens by making much easier their everyday contacts with public agencies and government services both at the national and local levels through new digital channels of political communication, should be regarded as a remarkable success of the ICT-driven public sector reforms. In this regard, the policy makers often refer to the achievements of the national e-government program in internal political debates and emphasize the importance of the current reforms in the sphere and, generally, the orthopraxy of the approaches that the national authorities have ostensibly chosen to apply in domestic politics. Therefore, the e-government area is usually prioritized as being crucial in the realization of many national strategic documents, thus, guaranteeing, to some extent, higher attention of the central and local governments to the topic with corresponding extensive media coverage and related public scrutiny. In fact, almost all ICT-driven public sector projects, ranging from e-governance and e-commerce to e-history and e-culture, are embedded today more or less in the e-government paradigm, making it a multidimensional phenomenon. In this regard, the launch of extremely popular e-government platforms such as e-application, e-taxation, e-learning, e-appointment, officials in social networks and many other projects help to maintain the positive image of the central government, since all of them are introduced and implemented at the national level, allowing all citizens to access the projects through a single e-government portal and receive the same set of information and interactive services, regardless of the regions they live in. The massive public relations campaign in the mass media increases the overall entourage around the initiatives.

One more important driver of the e-government movement lies in its role as a tool that helps to prevent indirectly the emergence of social tensions and conflicts. Along with notorious anti-corruption campaigns (OECD, 2014), sometimes, even against a number of senior officials with court hearings, related excessive public debates and emotional coverage and scrutiny in mass media, the introduction of the e-government projects and, more important, PR campaigns that usually accompany them, is designed to show not only the readiness of the central government to fight the most flagrant cases of bribery and embezzlement of budget funds but also the overall trend in transforming the entire system of public administration and public service, at least formally, toward less bureaucratic and more transparent models of functioning that ostensibly encourage collaboration, participation and engagement and intolerance to red tape and traditional closeness of administrative processes. In this respect, the online meetings of high-ranking officials with the public that are often organized on the portal of e-government both at the national and local levels, the active work of the government blog platforms as well as the media scrutiny over the activity of top politicians in social networks create a necessary atmosphere of digital communication and controllable political dialogue that help to smooth potential social tensions. The national authorities have always regarded social stability as a main public value and even advantage of the country, applying a wide range of administrative, financial and political measures to maintain it, and sometimes, even running to extremes on the road to keep the status quo, paying more attention in various reforms to the social and economic aspects of the national development and less to political ones. In this respect, e-government as *a politically neutral instrument* of public sector reforms in Kazakhstan, as long as it develops in a controllable administrative environment, ideally fits into the paradigm.

Key social drivers:

- Establishing new channels of communication with the public
- Making references to e-government achievements in social debates
- Controlling and preventing potential social conflicts in a digital manner

Key realization strategies:

- Introduction of one-stop shops and single e-government platforms
- Demonstrational anti-red tape and anti-corruption campaigns
- Extensive media coverage, propaganda campaigns and public debates

Key realization platforms:

- E-Application Project
- E-Learning Project
- E-Appointment Project
- Official Blog-Platform Project

Key stakeholders of e-government: analyzing the promising potential of the public-private partnership

The public sector: choosing a path of least effort

Like in many countries, in Kazakhstan, the public agencies play a crucial role in initiating and implementing a majority of the e-government projects, regarding such a monopolistic stance of the public sector in the promotion of the ICT-driven reforms as natural and normal. Therefore, such traditional ways to realize public sector reforms as directives and top-down administrative commands became the favorite and most often used instruments in promoting e-government politics, resulting in the creation of a super centralized model of its realization with such distinguishing features as a single implementation policy, single data storage and processing platforms, centralized authorization, etc. However, although there is a single operator of the e-government platform represented by the state-owned company – i.e. National Information Technologies – many departments both at the national and local levels of the Kazakh government participate in the development of various ICT-driven public sector projects and initiatives, realizing a multi-institutional nature of the phenomenon. In this regard, almost every ministry has at least one ICT-driven public sector project that is developed and maintained at the administrative level exclusively by its employees with some technical support from the single operator, which itself relies greatly on the data sets and information that come from the ministries, playing a main role in coordinating all e-government projects and services at the national level. For example, the Ministry for Investments and Development administers an innovative project such as the KZ Start, which, in turn, supports various independent third-party startups in the ICT sphere (The KZ Start Project, 2016). In total, of the 137 services that the ministry provides to citizens and businesses, 99 are rendered in digital format through a single platform of e-government (MIDK, 2016). In general, the following central government agencies develop various e-government projects and provide a wide range of e-services through the portal: Ministry of National Economy, Ministry of Finance, Ministry of Energy, Ministry of Civil Service Affairs, Ministry of Health and Social Development, Ministry of Foreign Affairs, Ministry of Internal Affairs, Ministry of Culture and Sport, Ministry of Defense, Ministry of Education and Science, Ministry of Agriculture and Ministry of Justice (see table 7.1).

Table 7.1 The specialized e-government projects of national government agencies

#	Government agencies	Specialized ICT-driven public projects	Popular e-government services
1	Ministry of National Economy	e-Trade project	• Assignment of housing benefits; • Obtainment of licenses
2	Ministry of Finance	e-Procurement project; e-Taxation project	• Advanced search of taxpayers; • Tax-debt review and payments
3	Ministry of Agriculture	e-Agriculture project	• Obtaining veterinary test protocols; • Obtaining veterinary certificates
4	Ministry of Investment and Development	KZ Start project	• Issuance of civil aircraft certificates; • Registration of small-size vessels
5	Ministry of Healthcare and Social Development	e-Health project	• Obtaining certificates on pension contributions; • Assignment of maternity and child care benefits
6	Ministry of Culture and Sport	e-Culture project; e-History project	• Issuance of archival references; • Issuance of permits for temporary export and import of cultural valuables

#	Government agencies	Specialized ICT-driven public projects	Popular e-government services
7	Ministry of Civil Service Affairs	e-Kyzmet project Anti-corruption project	• Civil service candidates testing; • Enlistment to the pool of the administrative civil service's candidates
8	Ministry of Education and Science	e-Learning project	• Child queuing for kindergartens; • Obtaining certificates on custodianship and guardianship
9	Ministry of Justice	e-Legislation project e-Notary project	• State registration of rights for real-estate objects; • Application for issuance of technical passports for real-estate objects

Source: own elaboration based on data from: The E-Notary Project (2015); The E-Taxation Project (2015); The Anticorruption Project (2016); The Cultural Heritage Project (2016); The e-Trade Project (2016); The Public e-Procurement Project (2016); The KZ Start Project (2016); MAK (2016); MCSAK (2016); MHSDK (2016); The e-Legislation Project (2016)

In addition, many regional and even local governments (*akimats*) develop and promote their own ICT projects and services through the single platform of e-government. In this regard, the development of the so-called e-*akimats* is one of the most popular forms to advance the concept at the local level. However, since many public electronic services are provided via the single national platform, many of the local projects do not offer a full range of digital products and *de facto* traditional websites that publish government information and data sets.

Main features of the public sector

Operational environment:

• E-government projects at the national, institutional and local levels realized mostly via a single digital platform

Key policy makers:

• Central government agencies and national ministries
• State-owned ICT companies and agencies
• Regional and local governments

Key incentives:

- Following global e-government, open government and e-participation trends
- Achieving domestic political, economic and social goals of the e-government policies
- Global country PR through the promotion of national e-government projects

Key tools of participation:

- Initiation of various public ICT-driven startups
- Funding of all e-government-related projects
- Realization of a single digital platform for all e-services
- Strict centralized control and administrative scrutiny

The nongovernmental sector: focusing on e-government consulting and global cooperation

The nongovernmental sector is beginning to play an ever-increasing role in promoting new dimensions in the development of the e-government concept in Kazakhstan such as open government, open data and e-participation. However, in comparison with the overwhelming political and administrative stance of the public sector in the sphere, the instruments of influence to which the NGOs could resort in this direction are usually limited to consultancy and co-funding of the various public ICT-driven projects. They often have to work in close cooperation with government agencies to achieve the goal. Also, it is necessary to note that both domestic and, more important, global nongovernmental stakeholders participate equally in the processes. In this regard, the organization of various master classes and brown bag seminars for the government stakeholders and private ICT developers became a popular form of concept promotion by foreign NGOs. Attracted by the increasing popularity of related open government projects launched by both government agencies and independent developers in Kazakhstan, they saw new opportunities to advance digital democracy in an unusual context of a typical developing and transitional country. Nonprofit and nongovernmental players universally well-known in the e-government sphere such as the Center for Open Data Enterprise, an international expert venue specializing in the promotion of open government (CODE, 2016); the Open Data 500, a global digital network of researchers that studies the impact of the *open data concept on democracy at the global level (* The Open Data 500, 2016); and many other organizations share their expertise and knowledge with various e-government policy makers and stakeholders in Kazakhstan during the forums, providing valuable technical and consultative help to an extremely wide range of the ICT-driven public projects in arranging various roundtables and classes (The E-Government of Kazakhstan, 2015). They have organized recently a number of unofficial meetings and lunches for local developers working in close partnership with government stakeholders in the sphere.

Main features of the nongovernmental sector

Operational environment:

- Official open government platforms
- Independent open data-driven projects

Key policy makers:

- Domestic nongovernmental organizations
- International nonprofit organizations and think tanks

Key incentives:

- Networking with e-government policy makers and independent ICT developers
- The promise of e-democracy and e-participation in the Central Asia region
- Promotion of open government and open data projects in an unusual cultural context

Key tools of participation:

- Co-organization and co-funding of various networking events and seminars
- Consultancy of public and private ICT-driven projects in the e-government sphere
- Popagation of the universal e-government values, realization mechanisms and trends

ICT developers: harnessing the promise of professional networking and collaboration

There are two types of ICT developers in Kazakhstan: the first group is directly associated with the public sector since the national government indirectly supervises the development of almost all e-government projects through a range of state-owned telecommunication companies and specialized semiprivate agencies, which themselves follow traditional double-tier bureaucratic subordination and administrative control and in fact represent government in the sphere. Many ICT agencies work in close cooperation with corresponding national ministries in developing their e-government projects, helping them to improve and advance various digital products and services. In this regard, semipublic developers such as the National Agency for Technological Development (NATD, 2015), the National Information Technologies Agency (NITEC, 2015) and Infocommunication Development Fund (ICT Fund, 2016) play an important role in promoting an extremely wide range of e-government projects at both national and local levels of governance. All of these agencies are politically and organizationally supervised by the Ministry of Investments and Development of Kazakhstan (MIDK, 2015) and Zerde National Infocommunication Holding, respectively. The latter administers several ICT-driven projects and startups (Zerde, 2015).

The second type of developer is a huge army of independent computer programmers, designers, coders, testers, students of the national technological universities, institutes and IT colleges and even technically savvy citizens, who find promising the active promotion of various open data and peer-to-peer projects in the e-government sphere and are generally driven by the virtue of professional curiosity, competition, enthusiasm and patriotism. In this regard, the emergence of various forums such as e-Government Hackathons (Manley, 2015), The Startup Battles Project (SBP, 2016) or multiple widespread Open Data Hack Days as well as numerous networking platforms and events such as The Tech Garden Project (TGP, 2016) and The Innovation Week (Kazakh TV, 2015) not only help to promote the concept among ICT developers but also provide great opportunities for professional networking among local computer specialists both with peers from other regions of the country and foreign IT experts, creating a reinvigorating environment of collaboration, participation and creativity in the sphere.

Main features of the ICT developers' participation

Operational environment:

- Open data-driven projects
- Wiki-based projects

Key stakeholders:

- Semipublic and private developers, designers and coders
- Students of the national technical universities and IT colleges
- Technically savvy citizens and foreign ICT experts

Key incentives:

- Professional curiosity among ICT experts
- Various contests and competition with peers
- Enthusiasm and patriotism among young developers

Key tools of participation:

- Knowledge sharing in wiki-based and e-participation projects
- Co-development in various open data-driven projects
- Consultancy of semipublic and private stakeholders
- Re-use of open data in various e-government startups

This promising environment of collaboration and public-private partnerships among the key stakeholders – i.e. government agencies, NGOs and ICT developers – helps to promote the e-government phenomenon into new dimensions, advancing potentially rewarding political and economic platforms such as open data-driven and e-participation startups. In this regard, social media begins to play an important role as a networking platform that helps to promote not only open professional cooperation in the sphere but also encourage the exchange of expertise and knowledge with peers from other regions of the planet. For example, various accounts of ICT developers in popular networking platforms such as Facebook, VKontakte, Google Plus, Twitter and GitHub as well as frequent organization of various hackathons and hack days (The HackDay Kazakhstan Project, 2015) and expert forums such as Ted^{x}Astana (The Tedxastana Project, 2015), Ted^{x}Almaty (The Tedxalmaty Project, 2016), The Week of Innovations (Kazinform, 2015b), the TechConnect and Open Data Conference (The Techconnect Project, 2015) and many other events are the most interesting venues to promote networking among IT professionals in the region. In partnership with global NGOs and think tanks, government officials often organize various brown bag seminars, online contests and master classes to share the new open data-driven culture among local computer specialists. This cooperation presumably helps to promote the e-government concept as an interesting and collaborative process beneficial for all stakeholders.

Key challenges of the e-government movement in Kazakhstan

Lack of internal institutional competition

One of the fundamental challenges in the overall development of e-government as a political concept is a lack of competition among the key stakeholders in the public sector, especially between central and regional authorities.

However, at first glance, obvious advantages such as the efficiency of a single realization strategy and convenience in maintaining single data sets, the reverse side of e-centralism in Kazakhstan, is a total administrative and financial control that the national authorities enjoy in the diffusion of the e-government concept at all levels of governance (Kassen, 2015), leaving almost no chance for the emergence of competitive regional projects in the area, which presumably would help to promote a healthy political competition between local authorities. As a result, the implementation of the vast majority of ICT-driven public sector initiatives happens at the national level and only if there is a strong political will and economic incentive to fund and develop such projects, not always taking into account the needs and recommendations of the local authorities in the related decision-making processes. As a result, they are usually passive in this respect. Moreover, because almost all e-government systems are realized as single national projects, they are by nature generic and over standardized.

The consequences of the lack of political competition are especially seen in the development of the open data sphere. In fact, although many open data-driven projects are realized today at the local level, mostly by independent developers and technically savvy citizens, the activity of the local authorities in promoting the concept is almost nonexistent, since the majority of data sets are published by the central public agencies and departments, which are experiencing greater administrative pressure from the national government. Therefore, the participation of the local governments is traditionally modest. In this regard, the development of official local open data projects and adoption of the corresponding amendments in the related regulatory acts such as e-government, open government laws and FOIAs would help to promote the open data concept at a much more effective level due to increased competition, participation and collaboration with other stakeholders, which is now required to implement successfully such startups. After all, open data as a new political dimension of e-government presumably should rely on civic engagement and collective wisdom of the local neighborhoods for its full realization.

Lack of constructive criticism and ideological opposition

One of the most fundamental challenges in the implementation of e-government projects is related to a lack of critical approach in the system of decision making to make the mechanism of its overall realization more controllable, transparent and, eventually, competitive. Kazakhstan is not unique in this respect, since the same situation with the realization of large ICT-driven public sector projects can be found in nearly any country in the world, regardless of whether developed or emerging. The institutional nature of the classic bureaucratic organization is not conducive for the development of constructive self-criticism, especially in public administration, regardless of cultural and regional contexts, without external factors of political pressure and scrutiny that should come from other stakeholders of the e-government movement. In this connection, the only way to solve the challenge is to promote greater public control in the sphere, which, in turn, demands a more active stance of the civil society and freedom of mass media. Moreover, the further development of the modern e-government system might require more collaborative ways to promote the concept where a single administrative control and public funding would presumably play a less important role than participation and cooperation of government with other stakeholders in building its more sustainable models, both in political and economic senses. In this regard, the development of open data and wiki-based technologies that advance civic engagement and e-participation is a promising harbinger of this trend in Kazakhstan and the movement in this direction should continue.

No participation of the business sector

One of the interesting aspects in the development of the e-government projects in Kazakhstan is a modest, almost nonexistent, participation of the local corporate sector in the sphere. Popular and effective instruments of collaboration with business stakeholders such as co-funding and co-development of various public ICT-driven projects – i.e. the movement that in many countries is mostly driven by philanthropic feelings, lobbying and image-making activities in promoting the initiatives and startups – is not a widespread trend in Kazakhstan. At first glance, the established mechanism of the single e-government administration and corresponding unilateral political support of the national authorities guarantees, to some extent, a favorable environment for the funding of the related projects from the national budget in the foreseeable future. In this respect, there is simply no need for fundraising and philanthropic activities, which, in any case, is not a popular movement, taking into account the fact that the role of the public sector in the sphere in Kazakhstan is overwhelming. However, it also implies that without financial support from the national budget, many of the projects in the e-government area could cease to exist, making the whole system of its implementation unsustainable and vulnerable to fundamental changes in the economic environment in the future, especially taking into account the lopsided nature of the national economy. Therefore, it is important to diversify the funding options and find a more sustainable financial model of the concept promotion in the public sector, partly through the engagement of local businesses and private corporations in the process.

Weak engagement of the local universities and think tanks

Another fundamental challenge in the e-government area is the fact that important players such as local educational and research centers are not fully engaged in the development of the concept in Kazakhstan. In fact, in many developed and some developing countries, both public and private universities as well as various think tanks actively participate in the promotion of related ICT-driven projects on a systematic basis and often in close cooperation with government agencies and various NGOs. Such private-public partnership is mutually beneficial, because the public stakeholders can outsource some of its functions to the nongovernmental sector, especially in developing conceptual models and testing scientifically proven realization strategies, while the latter receives new opportunities to participate in the processes and influence decision making in the area. In addition, various research centers could use this opportunity to diversify their fundraising options. Therefore, they could compete with each other for the scarce funding in the sphere, generating more effectively new ideas and advancing dramatically academic and practical expertise and knowledge. Today, the government agencies already engage specialists from various global educational institutions and universally well-known e-government centers – e.g. in organizing various master classes and brown bag seminars for the public and private stakeholders. However, it is also necessary to promote the creation and support of the e-government centers and think tanks at the national and local levels through various grants that would help to increase the domestic capacity in advancing research and development in the e-government sphere.

Inadequate regulation of information security and privacy issues

The development of large ICT-driven public sector projects as e-government and e-voting always causes concerns about information security of the technological systems that are used by the public agencies to operate them. In this regard, the most controversial aspects of criticism should be related to the authorization of citizens and use of digital signatures to access various interactive and transactional services. In Kazakhstan, the simple fact that all digital transactions are carried out at the national level in a universal manner, using single databases and processing centers, imposes a great responsibility on the e-government operators to maintain proper functioning of the entire system, because potential issues with information security could lead to massive leaks of confidential and private information and data, taking into account a strict centralized model of its realization. It is important to ensure an independent mechanism of external control and public scrutiny over the operation of various e-government systems. It should relate not only to the provision of public access to the systematic reports of the government agencies and actual technical documentation on regular tests and detailed logs of everyday operations of the mechanisms (Kassen, 2010) but also to the publication of information on names of companies and agencies that are engaged in the development of the related systems, ensuring a greater transparency in public procurement of the hardware and software. Therefore, all these measures of public control should be guaranteed in corresponding legal acts. In this regard, although some of the measures are stipulated in numerous regulatory documents adopted by the national parliament and president in previous years – e.g. in subsection 2 of the Conception of Information Security of Kazakhstan (2011) and Article 23 of the National Security Act of Kazakhstan (2012) – it could be also necessary to develop a special doctrine of multilevel information security explicitly in the e-government sphere that would help to ensure a more flexible and sophisticated mechanism of the government and public control over the operators and create additional technological and legal barriers against potential domestic and international intruders and unauthorized trespassers, taking into account the strategic importance of this national digital project (see figure 7.2).

The inertia in the public mentality

One of the most notoriously controversial aspects in the development of the e-government project in Kazakhstan is that despite the widespread diffusion of various interactive and transactional services, which for convenience are

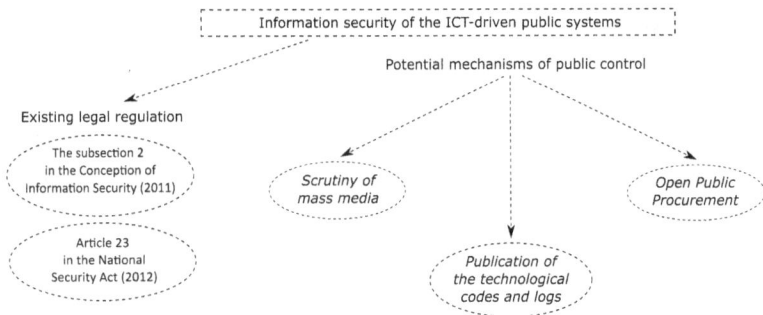

Figure 7.2 The existing and potential promising mechanisms of public control in the e-government sphere

Source: own illustration

provided online on a single digital platform, many citizens still prefer to receive government services in a traditional manner, visiting physically one-stop shops and meeting in person with the representatives of public agencies and affiliated structures. In fact, people usually need a limited number of documents and services from the government bodies and most of them are somehow related in Kazakhstan to property and social benefits topics such as the issue of certificates of legal address or pension contributions, which they could receive easily and quickly from the public centers and, more important, in a paper form. Paradoxically, both semipublic and private organizations that usually request the documents from citizens, often traditionally asking to present them as a paper certificate, even if it is just a printed version of the electronic document without stamps and handwritten signatures on it, given that both paper and electronic versions have the same unique verifiable identification number, therefore, negating the key advantage of the digital approach, since people have to resort to the printer anyway. In this regard, it is crucial to promote further the digital methods of the electronic document flow and control in the private sector, which itself dramatically falls behind in terms of informatization in comparison with the public sector, where the simultaneous exchange of digital documents among various agencies has become a widespread bureaucratic norm.

References

The Anticorruption Project (2016). http://anticorruption.gov.kz/
CODE (2016). The Center for Open Data Enterprise. http://opendataenterprise.org/index.html
The Conception of Information Security of Kazakhstan (2011, November 14). The Presidential Directive # 174. http://adilet.zan.kz/rus/docs/U1100000174
The Cultural Heritage Project (2016). http://www.madenimura.kz/en/
Damu (2015). The Presentation of a New Online Resource www.doingbusiness.gov.kz held in Almaty. http://www.damu.kz/17731
The E-Government of Kazakhstan (2015). www.egov.kz
The E-Legislation Project (2016). http://adilet.zan.kz/eng
The E-Notary Project (2015). http://enis.kz
The E-Taxation Project (2015). http://cabinet.salyk.kz
The E-Trade Project (2016). www.trade.gov.kz
The HackDay Kazakhstan Project (2015). http://hackday2015.kz/
Husain, M. A. M., Arezki, M. R., Breuer, M. P., Haksar, M. V., Helbling, M. T., Medas, P. A., . . . Sommer, M. (2015). *Global implications of lower oil prices* (No. 15). Washington, D.C.: International Monetary Fund.
ICT Fund (2016). Infocommunication Development Fund of Kazakhstan. www.ictfund.kz/about-fund?language=en
Kassen, M. (2010). *E-Government in Kazakhstan: Realization and prospects*, 6. Carbondale: Open SIUC, Southern Illinois University. http://opensiuc.lib.siu.edu/pnconfs_2010/6/

Kassen, M. (2015). *Understanding systems of e-Government: E-Federalism and e-Centralism in the United States and Kazakhstan.* Lanham, MD: Lexington Books.

The Kazakh TV channel (2015). http://kazakh-tv.kz

Kazinform (2015b). Week of Innovations to be held in Kazakhstan Nov 9–13, 2015. http://www.inform.kz/eng/article/2835333

The Kz Start Project (2016). The ICT-startups Accelerator Project. http://kzstart.kz/

MAK (2016). The Ministry of Agriculture of Kazakhstan. http://mgov.kz/

Manley, L. (2015). Open Data for Business in Kazakhstan. The World Bank. http://blogs.worldbank.org/opendata/open-data-business-kazakhstan

MCSAK (2016). The Ministry of Civil Service Affairs of Kazakhstan. http://kyzmet.gov.kz/ru/kategorii/o-deyatelnosti-ministerstva

MHSDK (2016). The Ministry of Healthcare and Social Development of Kazakhstan. http://www.mzsr.gov.kz/en/taxonomy/term/557

MIDK (2015). The Ministry of Investments and Development of Kazakhstan. http://www.mid.gov.kz/en

MIDK (2016). The Ministry for Investments and Development of Kazakhstan. http://mid.gov.kz/en/pages/public-services-provided-ministry-republic-kazakhstan-investment-and-development

NATD (2015). The National Agency of Technological Development. http://natd.gov.kz

The National Security Act of Kazakhstan (2012, January 6). The law of Kazakhstan # 427-IV. http://adilet.zan.kz/rus/docs/Z1200000527

NITEC (2015). http://www.nitec.kz/index.php/en

OECD (2014). Anti-Corruption Reforms in Kazakhstan. Monitoring of the Istanbul Anti-Corruption Action Plan.

The Open Data 500 (2016). http://www.opendata500.com

The Public e-Procurement Project (2016). http://goszakup.gov.kz

SBP(2016). The Startup Battles Projects. http://techconnect.tech/startup-competition/

Stier, S. (2015). Political determinants of e-government performance revisited: Comparing democracies and autocracies. *Government Information Quarterly*, *32*(3), 270–278.

The Techconnect Project (2015). http://techconnect.tech/blog/astex-2015-at-techconnect-astana

The Tedxastana Project (2015). http://tedxastana.com/

The Tedxalmaty Project (2016). www.tedxalmaty.com

TGP (2016). The Tech Garden Project http://techgarden.kz

The World Bank (2016). The Ease of Doing Business in Kazakhstan. http://www.doingbusiness.org/data/exploreeconomies/kazakhstan

Zerde (2015). The National Telecommunication Holding. www.zerde.gov.kz

Conclusion
Key findings, theoretical and practical contributions

The conclusion chapter presents generalizations on the key findings on the development of e-government in Kazakhstan and synthesis of materials presented in the previous chapters of the book, highlighting both theoretical and practical contributions.

Generalization of the key findings

Indeed, as all of these e-government projects demonstrate, Kazakhstan has achieved impressive results not only in advancing various ICT-driven public sector reforms but also in developing its global image as a promising experimental platform in terms of furthering its national e-government and e-participation initiatives in the developing world. The obvious *technological* and *economic* successes in this direction explain its steady progress in various prestigious and universally recognized rating lists and surveys that monitor the development of information society on a planetary scale, such as those that are organized and reexamined biannually by the United Nations and the World Bank. In this regard, the most important results it has achieved were in the e-participation subcategory of the survey. In 2012, Kazakhstan along with Singapore became second in this global competition, surprisingly outrunning many developed countries. This fact raised controversial discussions in the scientific communities about the elusive relationship between the development of e-government projects, which are based on presumably collaborative and participatory platforms, and progress in promoting digital democracy in many emerging countries. In this regard, one of the interesting findings of the case study research is that the development of the official e-government platforms provide promising opportunities to promote civic engagement and mutually beneficial cooperation between government and civil society in the public sector, but does not change the fundamental basis of the political system or advances traditional democratic institutions in a typical developing and post-totalitarian context.

Another important finding is that despite the presumably collaborative conceptual nature of the open government paradigm, in reality the traditional top-down directives and administrative commands could be paradoxically effective in promoting various public platforms in the sphere even in a less collaborative political culture. Furthermore, the unitary administrative context in the adoption of the e-participation philosophy is conducive for the development of all public sector projects in the e-government sphere on a single technological platform, while the lack of regulation and inconsistency in the promotion of the e-participation movement can result in the emergence of new phenomena such as electronic bureaucracy.

The adherence of the policy makers to classic yet effective black-box tools of public sector reforms such as traditional executive directives, top-down administrative commands and centralized public funding, especially in launching a wide range of transactional services for both citizens and businesses, has allowed them to achieve impressive results in the sphere, which eventually helped to universally propagate the nation as a promising model to follow for other developing countries. However, the realization of the national e-participation projects has been carried out un-homogenously, especially in relationship to the advancement of important collaborative components, exposing some fundamentally new challenges that Kazakhstan is experiencing today in the e-government area such as the controversial effects of the post-totalitarian public mindset, the lack of a regulatory basis in the sphere and, most important, the lack of political culture conducive to the emergence of strong civil society – i.e. in the dimensions of e-government where the established mechanisms of the top-down implementation do not work anymore. In this regard, it is important to focus on more effective and sophisticated civic engagement platforms in promoting e-participation among all members of the society.

Theoretical contributions

The primary theoretical contribution of the research lies in the analysis of its unusual cultural context that distinguishes the case of Kazakhstan in the traditional e-government academic literature. In contrast to the general trend in the scientific works that focus mostly on researching the diffusion of the e-government phenomenon in the developed countries of the world, paying less attention to the emerging and, more important, transitional economies, the investigation presented in the book is partly aimed at closing the gap in the research and enriching the academic literature with new evidence and findings about the development of the concept in *sui generis* conditions of the developing economy. In this regard, as a typical emerging and post-totalitarian nation, Kazakhstan has the right combination of unique cultural, economic and political characteristics that makes it an interesting example for case study research. In an attempt to generate new knowledge about the indirect impact of these unusual contexts on the advance of e-government as a multidimensional political and socioeconomic concept, the author tried to understand how such as a presumably universal tool of public sector reform works in this emerging nation.

Another theoretical contribution of the work is a presentation of its arguably more universal research framework in comparison with previously used analytical approaches that could be valuable in investigating the promotion of the e-government phenomenon in other developing, transitional and post-totalitarian economies, enriching the existing theoretical models that are usually utilized in related case study research. In this regard, aspects of the analysis presented in the work such as *a multidimensional approach* that includes the investigation of the e-government phenomenon from a range of perspectives such as *a country context analysis* that studies the implications of the national geography, history, political and social systems, economy, public administration, telecommunication industry, nongovernmental sector, mass media and even foreign policy on the development of the phenomenon in Kazakhstan; *a retrospective analysis* that focuses on studying the gradual evolution and transformation of the e-government concept toward the open government domain of the idea; *a content analysis* that investigates the key e-government projects realized at the national level; and, finally, *a policy analysis* that speculates on the apparitional emergence of the open government and e-participation phenomena in Kazakhstan. These results could help researchers in investigating the development of the e-government institutions in other emerging and transitional countries in all their diversity.

Practical contributions

The main practical contribution of the book is providing a close and detailed policy review of the e-government politics in Kazakhstan that could be especially helpful for policy makers and practitioners in evaluating and improving the work of various ICT-driven public sector projects in the sphere. In this regard, the investigation of promising e-government initiatives and startups such as the *E-Application Project* that is aimed at de-bureaucratizing the entire public administration mechanism, the *official government social media and blog platforms* that play an important role in maintaining domestic public relations and attracting the attention of mass media to the e-government concept, the *E-Procurement Project* that helps to ensure greater transparency of public spending, the *E-Appointment System* that generates heated disputes about the emergence of new phenomena such as e-bureaucracy and digital red tape, the *E-Licensing Project* that opens new promising aspects to promote the public-private partnership in the sphere, the *E-Payment Platform* that creates new dimensions for the development of e-commerce in the e-government-related transactions, the *E-Taxation System* that dramatically changes the fundamentals of the government-business relationship in the sphere, the *one-stop shop project* that might be regarded as a physical representation of the single e-government realization policy at the local levels, the *E-Learning Project* that raises new questions about the extreme expensiveness of the national e-government initiatives in the education sphere, the *mobile e-government project* that opens new dimensions for the promotion of the concept at the national and local levels and, finally, the *E-Notary Project* that provides a promising platform to improve the operation of the business in a digital manner, could be useful as analytical material in the work of e-government entrepreneurs and policy makers.

Another practical contribution of the research is a number of recommendations that the author presents in his work for e-government practitioners and project managers in solving various challenges and issues in a wide range of digital platforms and initiatives realized in Kazakhstan at the national and local levels of governance. In this regard, Chapter 2, Chapter 5 and Chapter 6 provide a concrete set of suggestions on how to improve administratively and politically the operation of various e-government and, more important, open government initiatives such as open lawmaking, open dialogue and open data projects. The author also indicates the potential emergence of new challenges that may impede the development of the concept in Kazakhstan such as the lack of the institutional competition among its key stakeholders in government; ubiquitous flattery and lack of constructive criticism in the political system and public administration; no collaboration with the business sector, local universities and think tanks in promoting the concept; weak regulation of the e-government sphere, especially in mitigating the gaps in information security; and finally, the inertia of the public mentality and old bureaucratic machine and the author offers practical recommendations on how to overcome them.

Bibliography

Abdrazak, P. K., & Musa, K. S. (2015). The impact of the cosmodrome "Baikonur" on the environment and human health. *International Journal of Biology and Chemistry, 9*(1), 26–29.

The Adilet Open Laws Project (2015). http://adilet.zan.kz/eng

Ak Orda (2007). President Nursultan Nazarbayev Is Going to Hold an Internet-Conference on the 7th of June, 2007 and to Answer Questions of Users of the Global Network. http://www.akorda.kz/pda.php/en/page/page_glava-gosudarstva-nursultan-nazarbaev-7-iyunya-etogo-goda-provedet-internet-konf_1348723518

Al-Khamayseh, S., Lawrence, E., & Zmijewska, A. (2006). Towards understanding success factors in interactive mobile government. Paper presented at the Proceedings of Euro mGov 2006: The Second European Conference on Mobile Government, Brighton, UK.

Amailef, K., & Lu, J. (2013). Ontology-supported case-based reasoning approach for intelligent m-government emergency response services. *Decision Support Systems, 55*(1), 79–97.

The Anticorruption Project (2016). http://anticorruption.gov.kz/

Arora, S. (2008). National e-ID card schemes: A European overview. *Information Security Technical Report, 13*(2), 46–53.

Åström, J., Karlsson, M., Linde, J., & Pirannejad, A. (2012). Understanding the rise of e-participation in non-democracies: Domestic and international factors. *Government Information Quarterly, 29*(2), 142–150.

Bader, M. (2011). Hegemonic political parties in post-Soviet Eurasia: Towards party-based authoritarianism? *Communist and Post-Communist Studies, 44*(3), 189–197.

Baldoni, R. (2012). Federated identity management systems in e-government: The case of Italy. *Electronic Government, an International Journal, 9*(1), 64–84.

Bellio, E., & Buccoliero, L. (2013). Citizen web empowerment across Italian cities: A benchmarking approach. In C. Silva (Ed.)., *Citizen E-Participation in Urban Governance: Crowdsourcing and Collaborative Creativity* (pp. 284–302). Hershey, PA: Information Science Reference.

Berntzen, L., & Olsen, M. G. (2009, February). Benchmarking e-government-a comparative review of three international benchmarking studies. In *Digital Society, 2009. ICDS'09. Third International Conference on* (pp. 77–82). New York: IEEE.

Bertot, J. C., Jaeger, P. T., & Grimes, J. M. (2010). Using ICTs to create a culture of transparency: E-government and social media as openness and anti-corruption tools for societies. *Government Information Quarterly, 27*(3), 264–271.

Bhuiyan, S. H. (2010). E-government in Kazakhstan: Challenges and its role to development. *Public Organization Review, 10*(1), 31–47.

Bhuiyan, S. H. (2011a). Trajectories of e-government implementation for public sector service delivery in Kazakhstan. *International Journal of Public Administration, 34*(9), 604–615.

Bhuiyan, S. H. (2011b). Transition towards a knowledge-based society in post-communist Kazakhstan: Does good governance matter? *Journal of Asian and African Studies, 46*(4), 404–421.

Bhuiyan, S. H., & Amagoh, F. (2011). Public sector reform in Kazakhstan: Issues and perspectives. *International Journal of Public Sector Management, 24*(3), 227–249.

Bowyer, A. C. (2008). *Parliament and political parties in Kazakhstan.* Washington, D.C.: Central Asia-Caucasus Institute & Silk Road Studies Program, Johns Hopkins University-SAIS..

Brown, B. (1990). The public role in perestroika in central Asia. *Central Asian Survey, 9*(1), 87–96.

Carlsen, L., Kenessov, B. N., Batyrbekova, S. Y., & Nauryzbaev, M. K. (2010). On the space activities at the Baikonur cosmodrome: An approach to an integrated environmental assessment. *International Journal of Environmental Sciences, 1*, 55–64.

Carter, L., & Bélanger, F. (2005). The utilization of e-government services: Citizen trust, innovation and acceptance factors. *Information Systems Journal, 15*(1), 5–25.

Castells, M. (2015). *Networks of outrage and hope: Social movements in the internet age.* Hoboken: John Wiley & Sons.

Cegarra-Navarro, J. G., Pachón, J. R. C., & Cegarra, J. L. M. (2012). E-government and citizen's engagement with local affairs through e-websites: The case of Spanish municipalities. *International Journal of Information Management, 32*(5), 469–478.

The Center for Engineering and Transfer of Technologies (CETT) (2015). http://www.cett.kz/

The Center of Government Efficiency Evaluation (2014). http://www.bagalau.kz/ru/med/smi/i224

Chadwick, A., & May, C. (2003). Interaction between states and citizens in the age of the internet: "E-government" in the United States, Britain, and the European Union. *Governance-Oxford, 16*(2), 271–300.

Chen, Y. N., Chen, H. M., Huang, W., & Ching, R. K. (2006). E-government strategies in developed and developing countries: An implementation framework and case study. *Journal of Global Information Management, 14*(1), 23–46.

Chesbrough, H. (2010). Business model innovation: Opportunities and barriers. *Long Range Planning, 43*(2), 354–363.

Ciurana, E. (2009). *Developing with google app engine.* New York: Apress.

The Center for Open Data Enterprise (CODE) (2016). http://opendataenterprise.org/index.html

The Committee of Transport (2015). The Committee of Transport in the Ministry of Investments and Development of Kazakhstan. http://transport.mid.gov.kz/ru

The Conception of Information Security of Kazakhstan (2011, November 14). The Presidential Directive # 174. http://adilet.zan.kz/rus/docs/U1100000174

The Cultural Heritage Project (2016). http://www.madenimura.kz/en/

Cummings, S. N. (2003). Eurasian bridge or murky waters between east and west? Ideas, identity and output in Kazakhstan's foreign policy. *Journal of Communist Studies and Transition Politics*, *19*(3), 139–155.

Damu (2015). The Presentation of a New Online Resource www.doingbusiness.gov. kz held in Almaty. http://www.damu.kz/17731

Davies, T. G., & Bawa, Z. A. (2012). The promises and perils of open government data (OGD). *The Journal of Community Informatics*, *8*(2). http://www.ci-journal. net/index.php/ciej/article/view/929/955

De Clercq, J. (2002). Single sign-on architectures. In G. I. Davida, Y. Frankel & O. Rees (Eds.), *Infrastructure security* (pp. 40–58). Berlin Heidelberg: Springer.

The Decree N 88-b (2005, April 5). The rules for the registration of the domain space in the Kazakhstan segment of the Internet. The decree of the Acting Chairman of the Informatization and Communication Agency of Kazakhstan.

Diachenko, S. (2008). *The government and NGOs in Kazakhstan: Strategy, forms, and mechanisms of cooperation.* Sweden: CA&CC Press.

Diener, A. C. (2002). National territory and the reconstruction of history in Kazakhstan. *Eurasian Geography and Economics*, *43*(8), 632–650.

The Directive N 464 (2013, January 8). The State Program "Information Kazakhstan – 2020". http://adilet.zan.kz/rus/docs/U1300000464#z0

The Directive N 958 (2010, March 19). The Forced Industrial and Innovation Development of Kazakhstan in 2010–2014. http://adilet.zan.kz/rus/docs/U100000958_

The E-Application System (2015). http://egov.kz/wps/portal/Content?contentPath=/ egovcontent/citizensgovernment/articlesforcg/passport/e_app&lang=ru

The E-Appointment System (2015). http://egov.kz/wps/portal/Content?content Path=/egovcontent /citizensgovernment/ articlesforcg/passport/online_admission &lang=ena

ECC (2015). The Electronic Commerce Center. http://ecc.kz/en

The E-Culture Project (2015). http://www.madenimura.kz/en/

The E-Government Directive # 1471 (2004). The State Program of E-Government Formation in Kazakhstan for 2005–2007 (2004, November 10). The Presidential Directive. http://adilet.zan.kz/rus/docs/U040001471_

The E-Government of Kazakhstan (2015). www.egov.kz

The E-History Project (2015). http://e-history.kz/en

Eisenhardt, K. M. (1989). Building theories from case study research. *Academy of Management Review*, *14*(4), 532–550.

The E-Learning Project (2015). http://e.edu.kz

The Electronic Address Platform (2014). http://egov.kz/wps/portal/citizensGovernment

The E-Legislation Project (2016). http://adilet.zan.kz/eng

The E-Licensing Project (2015). http://elicense.kz

Emrich-Bakenova, S. (2009). Trajectory of civil service development in Kazakhstan: Nexus of politics and administration. *Governance*, *22*(4), 717–745.

The E-Notary Project (2015). http://enis.kz

The E-Payment Project (2015). www.epay.gov.kz

The E-Procurement Law (2007, July 21). N 303-III. http://adilet.zan.kz/rus/docs/
Z070000303_

The E-Taxation Project (2015). http://cabinet.salyk.kz

The E-Trade Project (2016). www.trade.gov.kz

Evans, A. M., & Campos, A. (2013). Open government initiatives: Challenges
of citizen participation. *Journal of Policy Analysis and Management, 32*(1),
172–185.

Fan, B., & Luo, J. (2014). Benchmarking scale of e-government stage in Chinese
municipalities from government chief information officers' perspective. *Information
Systems and E-Business Management, 12*(2), 259–284.

The Freedom of Information Act (2015, November 16). The Kazakh Law on
Access to Information. Law # 401-V (2015). http://online.zakon.kz/Document/?
doc_id=39415981

Google Trends (2015). www.google.com/trends

The Government Resolution N 1155–1 (2007, November 30). The Program of
E-Government Formation in Kazakhstan for 2008–2010. http://adilet.zan.kz/rus/
docs/P0700011551

The HackDay Kazakhstan Project (2015). http://hackday2015.kz/

Hardy, C. A., & Williams, S. P. (2008). E-government policy and practice: A theoretical and empirical exploration of public e-procurement. *Government Information Quarterly, 25*(2), 155–180.

Harrison, T. M., Guerrero, S., Burke, G. B., Cook, M., Cresswell, A., Helbig, N.,
. . . Pardo, T. (2011, June). Open government and e-government: Democratic
challenges from a public value perspective. In *Proceedings of the 12th Annual
International Digital Government Research Conference: Digital Government
Innovation in Challenging Times* (pp. 245–253). College Park, MD: ACM.

Hindley, B. (2008). *Kazakhstan and the world economy: An assessment of Kazakhstan's trade policy and pending accession to the WTO.* Brussels: European Centre
for International Political Economy.

Hung, S. Y., Chang, C. M., & Kuo, S. R. (2013). User acceptance of mobile
e-government services: An empirical study. *Government Information Quarterly,
30*(1), 33–44.

Husain, M. A. M., Arezki, M. R., Breuer, M. P., Haksar, M. V., Helbling, M. T.,
Medas, P. A., . . . Sommer, M. (2015). *Global implications of lower oil prices*
(No. 15). Washington, D.C.: International Monetary Fund.

IBP USA (2009). *Kazakhstan company laws and regulations handbook* (Vol. 1).
Strategic Information and Regulations. Washington, D.C.: International Business
Publications.

ICT Fund (2016). Infocommunication Development Fund of Kazakhstan. www.
ictfund.kz/about-fund?language=en

IITU (2015). The International Information Technology University. www.iitu.kz

The International Telecommunication Union (2015). https://itunews.itu.int/En/3946-
Electronic-licensing-in-Kazakhstan.note.aspx

The Internet-Conference Platform (2014). http://egov.kz/wps/portal/conference

The Internet-Conference Platform (2015). http://egov.kz/wps/portal/conference?lang=ru
The Internet Statistics of Kazakhstan (2015). www.zero.kzInternews Kazakhstan (2015). http://www.internews.kz/
Isaacs, R. (2011). *Party system formation in Kazakhstan: Between formal and informal Politics* (Vol. 26). London and New York: Routledge.
Islam, M. S. (2008). Towards a sustainable e-Participation implementation model. *European Journal of ePractice, 5*(10), 1–12.
Janenova, S. (2009). One stop shop in Kazakhstan: Breaking-up traditional bureaucracy or a new look for old practice. In *Open Society Institute/Local Government Initiative Fellowship, Conference Paper.*
Janenova, S. (2010). E-Government in Kazakhstan: Challenges for a transitional country. In *18th NISPAcee Annual Conference "Public Administration in Times of Crisis"* (pp. 12–14). Warsaw, Poland.
Janssen, M., Charalabidis, Y., & Zuiderwijk, A. (2012). Benefits, adoption barriers and myths of open data and open government. *Information Systems Management, 29*(4), 258–268.
Jäppinen, S., Toivonen, T., & Salonen, M. (2013). Modelling the potential effect of shared bicycles on public transport travel times in Greater Helsinki: An open data approach. *Applied Geography, 43*, 13–24.
Johnson, E., & Kolko, B. (2010). e-Government and transparency in authoritarian regimes: Comparison of national-and city-level e-government web sites in Central Asia. *Digital Icons: Studies in Russian, Eurasian and Central European New Media, 3*, 15–48.
Kahate, A. (2013). *Cryptography and network security.* New Delhi: Tata McGraw-Hill Education.
Kassen, M. (2010). *E-Government in Kazakhstan: Realization and prospects*, 6. Carbondale: Open SIUC, Southern Illinois University. http://opensiuc.lib.siu.edu/pnconfs_2010/6/
Kassen, M. (2012). *Empowering social media: Citizens-source e-Government and peer-to-peer networks*, 3. Carbondale: Open SIUC, Southern Illinois University. http://opensiuc.lib.siu.edu/pnconfs_2012/3/
Kassen, M. (2013). A promising phenomenon of open data: A case study of the Chicago open data project. *Government Information Quarterly, 30*(4), 508–513.
Kassen, M. (2014). Globalization of e-government: Open government as a global agenda; benefits, limitations and ways forward. *Information Development, 30*(1), 51–58.
Kassen, M. (2015). *Understanding systems of e-Government: E-Federalism and E-Centralism in the United States and Kazakhstan.* Lanham, MD: Lexington Books.
The Kazakh Agency of Statistics (2015). http://www.stat.gov.kz
Kazakhtelecom (2015). www.telecom.kz/en
The Kazakh TV channel (2015). http://kazakh-tv.kz
Kazinform (2015a). http://www.inform.kz/rus/article/2818035
Kazinform (2015b, November 9–13). Week of Innovations to be held in Kazakhstan. http://www.inform.kz/eng/article/2835333
KazPost (2015). www.kazpost.kz

KazSatNet (2015). www.kazsatnet.kz

Kendirbaeva, G. (1997). Migrations in Kazakhstan: Past and present. *Nationalities Papers, 25*(4), 741–751.

Kenny, T., & Gross, P. (2008). Journalism in Central Asia: A victim of politics, economics, and widespread self-censorship. *The International Journal of Press/Politics, 13*(4), 515–525.

Kjærnet, H., Satpaev, D., & Torjesen, S. (2008, February). Big business and high-level politics in Kazakhstan: An everlasting symbiosis? *The China and Eurasia Forum Quarterly, 6*(1), 95–107.

Knox, C. (2008). Kazakhstan: Modernizing government in the context of political inertia. *International Review of Administrative Sciences, 74*(3), 477–496.

Kushchu, I. (2007). *Mobile government: An emerging direction in e-Government.* USA: Hershey, PA: IGI Publishing.

Kushchu, I., & Kuscu, H. (2003, July). From e-government to m-government: Facing the inevitable. In *The 3rd European Conference on E-Government* (pp. 253–260). MCIL Trinity College, Dublin, Ireland.

Kutan, A. M., & Wyzan, M. L. (2005). Explaining the real exchange rate in Kazakhstan, 1996–2003: Is Kazakhstan vulnerable to the Dutch disease? *Economic Systems, 29*(2), 242–255.

The Kz Start Project (2016). The ICT-startups Accelerator Project. http://kzstart.kz/

Lathrop, D., & Ruma, L. (2010). *Open government: Collaboration, transparency, and participation in practice.* Sebastopol, CA: O'Reilly Media, Inc.

Lee, S. M., Tan, X., & Trimi, S. (2005). Current practices of leading e-government countries. *Communications of the ACM, 48*(10), 99–104.

Linde, J., & Karlsson, M. (2013). The dictator's new clothes: The relationship between e-participation and quality of government in non-democratic regimes. *International Journal of Public Administration, 36*(4), 269–281.

Linders, D. (2012). From e-government to we-government: Defining a typology for citizen coproduction in the age of social media. *Government Information Quarterly, 29*(4), 446–454.

Luong, P. J., & Weinthal, E. (1999). The NGO paradox: Democratic goals and non-democratic outcomes in Kazakhstan. *Europe-Asia Studies, 51*(7), 1267–1284.

Lyon, D. (2005). The border is everywhere: ID cards, surveillance and the other. In E. Zureik & M. B. Salter (Eds.), *Global surveillance and policing: Borders, security, identity*, Vol. 5 (pp. 66–82). Portland, OR: Willan Publishing.

Lyon, D. (2009). *Identifying citizens: ID cards as surveillance.* Malden, MA: Polity Press.

MAK (2016). The Ministry of Agriculture of Kazakhstan. http://mgov.kz/

Manley, L. (2015). Open Data for Business in Kazakhstan. The World Bank. http://blogs.worldbank.org/opendata/open-data-business-kazakhstan

Marat, E. (2009). Nation branding in Central Asia: A new campaign to present ideas about the state and the nation. *Europe-Asia Studies, 61*(7), 1123–1136.

McGlinchey, E., & Johnson, E. (2007). Aiding the Internet in central Asia. *Democratisation, 14*(2), 273–288.

McKenzie, R., Crompton, M., & Wallis, C. (2008). Use cases for identity management in e-government. *IEEE Security & Privacy, 6*(2), 51–57.

MCSAK (2016). The Ministry of Civil Service Affairs of Kazakhstan. http://kyzmet. gov.kz/ru/kategorii/o-deyatelnosti-ministerstva

Melvin, N. J. (2009). The European Union, Kazakhstan and the 2010 OSCE Chairmanship. *Security and Human Rights, 20*(1), 42–47.

MHSDK (2016). The Ministry of Healthcare and Social Development of Kazakhstan. http://www.mzsr.gov.kz/en/taxonomy/term/557

Micklin, P. (2007). The Aral sea disaster. *Annual Review of Earth and Planetary Sciences, 35*, 47–72.

MIDK (2015). The Ministry of Investments and Development of Kazakhstan. http://www.mid.gov.kz/en

MIDK (2016). The Ministry for Investments and Development of Kazakhstan. http://mid.gov.kz/en/pages/public-services-provided-ministry-republic-kazakhstan-investment-and-development

MJK (2015). The Ministry of Justice of Kazakhstan. www.adilet.gov.kz/en

MNEK (2015). The Ministry of the National Economy. http://economy.gov.kz/en/

The Mobile Government of Kazakhstan (2015). http://egov.kz/wps/portal/Content?contentPath=/egovcontent/transports/communications/article/mobile_goverment&lang=ru

Moon, M. J. (2002). The evolution of e-government among municipalities: Rhetoric or reality? *Public Administration Review, 62*(4), 424–433.

Mouraviev, N., Kakabadse, N., & Robinson, I. (2012). Concessionary nature of public-private partnerships in Russia and Kazakhstan: A critical review. *International Journal of Public Administration, 35*(6), 410–420.

NATD (2015). The National Agency of Technological Development. http://natd. gov.kz

The National Security Act of Kazakhstan (2012, January 6). The law of Kazakhstan # 427-IV. http://adilet.zan.kz/rus/docs/Z1200000527

NITEC (2015). http://www.nitec.kz/index.php/en

Obama, B. (2009). Memorandum for the heads of executive departments and agencies. *Presidential Studies Quarterly, 39*(3), 429.

Obi, T., & Iwasaki, N. (Eds.). (2015). *A decade of world e-government rankings* (Vol. 7). Amsterdam: IOS Press.

OECD (2007). *Fighting corruption in transition economies: Kazakhstan 2007.* Paris: OECD Publishing.

OECD (2014). *Anti-corruption reforms in Kazakhstan.* Monitoring of the Istanbul Anti-Corruption Action Plan. Paris: OECD Publishing.

The Official Blog-Platform in the Kostanay Region (2015). http://akim.blogs.kostanay.gov.kz

The Official Blog-Platform in the Pavlodar Region (2015). http://blog.pavlodar.gov.kz/

The Official Blog-Platform of Government Executives (2015). http://www.blogs. e.gov.kz/en

The Officials in Social Networks Project (2014). http://egov.kz/wps/portal/Content?contentPath=/egovcontent/citizensgovernment/articlesforcg/passport/off_twi&lang=en

Ohayon, I. (2013). The Kazakh famine: The beginnings of sedentarization. *Mass Violence & Resistance: An Interdisciplinary Online Journal.* Paris: The Paris Institute of

Political Studies. http://www.sciencespo.fr/mass-violence-war-massacre-resistance/en/document/kazakh-famine-beginnings-sedentarization

Olcott, M. B. (1981). The collectivization drive in Kazakhstan. *Russian Review*, *40*(2), 122–142.

The Online Conference Platform (2015). http://egov.kz/wps/portal/conference?lang=ru

The Open Data 500 (2016). http://www.opendata500.com

The Open Data Project (2013). http://data.egov.kz/

The Open Government Partnership (2015). http://www.opengovpartnership.org/

The Open Government Project (2015). http://open.egov.kz/

The Open Lawmaking Platform (2015). http://legalacts.egov.kz/

Ospanova, S. (2015, April 7). Kazakhstani postmen to be provided with smartphones. *Kazpravda Newspaper.* http://www.kazpravda.kz/en/rubric/society/kazakhstani-postmen-to-be-provided-with-smartphones/

Otjacques, B., Hitzelberger, P., & Feltz, F. (2007). Interoperability of e-government information systems: Issues of identification and data sharing. *Journal of Management Information Systems, 23*(4), 29–51.

Perlman, B. J., & Gleason, G. (2007). Cultural determinism versus administrative logic: Asian values and administrative reform in Kazakhstan and Uzbekistan. *International Journal of Public Administration, 30*(12–14), 1327–1342.

Pianciola, N. (2001). The collectivization famine in Kazakhstan, 1931–1933. *Harvard Ukrainian Studies, 25*(3/4), 237–251.

Polian, P. M. (2004). *Against their will: The history and geography of forced migrations in the USSR*. Budapest and New York: Central European University Press.

The Public Discussion Platform (2014). http://egov.kz/wps/portal/ContentDiscussion

The Public e-Procurement Project (2015). http://www.goszakup.gov.kz/

The Public Service Centers Project (2015). http://con.gov.kz/

Raballand, G. (2003). Determinants of the negative impact of being landlocked on trade: An empirical investigation through the Central Asian case. *Comparative Economic Studies, 45*(4), 520–536.

RCLI (2015). The Republican Center of Legal Information. http://www.rkao.kz

Reddick, C. G., & Roy, J. (2013). Business perceptions and satisfaction with e-government: Findings from a Canadian survey. *Government Information Quarterly, 30*(1), 1–9.

Resolution N 369 (2014, April 17). On the Agency of Informatization and Communication of Kazakhstan. http://adilet.zan.kz/rus/docs/P1400000369#z12

Resolution N 479 (2005). On Approval of the Development of the Joint-stock Company Kazakhtelecom for 2005–2007. Resolution of the Government of the Republic of Kazakhstan dated May 19, 2005 N 479"

Resolution N 983 (2010, September 29). The Program of the Information and Communication Technology Development in Kazakhstan for 2010–2014. http://adilet.zan.kz/rus/docs/P100000983_

Reuters (2007). Kazakhs Shower President with Cryptic Questions. http://www.reuters.com/article/2007/06/01/us-kazakhstan-webcast-idUSL0131903220070601

Rorissa, A., Demissie, D., & Pardo, T. (2011). Benchmarking e-government: A comparison of frameworks for computing e-government index and ranking. *Government Information Quarterly, 28*(3), 354–362.

Rustemova, A. (2011). Political economy of Central Asia: Initial reflections on the need for a new approach. *Journal of Eurasian Studies*, *2*(1), 30–39.

SBP(2016). The Startup Battles Projects. http://techconnect.tech/startup-competition/

Schatz, E. (2008). Transnational image making and soft authoritarian Kazakhstan. *Slavic Review*, *67*(1), 50–62.

Schwegmann, C. (2013). Open data in developing countries. *European Public Sector Information Platform Topic Report* (2013/02).

Shareef, M. A., Archer, N., & Dwivedi, Y. K. (2012). Examining adoption behavior of mobile government. *The Journal of Computer Information Systems*, *53*(2), 39.

Simon, S. L., Baverstock, K. F., & Lindholm, C. (2003). A summary of evidence on radiation exposures received near to the Semipalatinsk nuclear weapons test site in Kazakhstan. *Health Physics*, *84*(6), 718–725.

Soros Foundation (2015). www.ru.soros.kz

Stier, S. (2015). Political determinants of e-government performance revisited: Comparing democracies and autocracies. *Government Information Quarterly*, *32*(3), 270–278.

Takada, J., Hoshi, M., Nagatomo, T., Yamamoto, M., Endo, S., Takatsuji, T., . . . Tchaijunusova, N. J. (1999). External doses of residents near Semipalatinsk nuclear test site. *Journal of Radiation Research*, *40*(4), 337–344.

Tat Kei Ho, A. (2002). Reinventing local governments and the e-government initiative. *Public Administration Review*, *62*(4), 434–444.

The Techconnect Project (2015). http://techconnect.tech/blog/astex-2015-at-tech connect-astana

The Tedxalmaty Project (2016). www.tedxalmaty.com

The Tedxastana Project (2015). http://tedxastana.com/

Tengrinews (2011). http://en.tengrinews.kz/edu/Almost-1-billion-allocated-for-e-learning-in-Kazakhstan-4092/

Terry, V. (2005). Postcard from the Steppes: A snapshot of public relations and culture in Kazakhstan. *Public Relations Review*, *31*(1), 31–36.

TGP (2016). The Tech Garden Project. http://techgarden.kz

The United Nations Radio (2015). http://www.unmultimedia.org/radio/russian/archives/203611/

UNPAN (2003). The Global E-Government Survey. United Nations Public Administration Network. http://unpan3.un.org/egovkb/en-us/Reports/UN-E-Government-Survey-2003

UNPAN (2004). Global E-Government Readiness Report. Towards Access for Opportunity. http://unpan1.un.org/intradoc/groups/public/documents/un/unpan019207.pdf

UNPAN (2005). UN Global E-government Readiness Report. From E-Government to e-Inclusion. http://unpan1.un.org/intradoc/groups/public/documents/un/unpan021888.pdf

UNPAN (2008). UN Global E-Government Survey. From E-Government to Connected Governance. http://unpan1.un.org/intradoc/groups/public/documents/un/unpan028607.pdf

UNPAN (2010). The Global E-Government Survey. Leveraging E-government at a Time of Financial and Economic Crisis. http://www2.unpan.org/egovkb/global_reports/10report.htm

UNPAN (2012). The Global E-Government Survey. E-Government for the People. http://unpan3.un.org/egovkb/Portals/egovkb/Documents/un/2012-Survey/unpan048065.pdf

UNPAN (2014). The Global E-Government Survey. E-Government for the Future We Want. http://unpan3.un.org/egovkb/Reports/UN-E-Government-Survey-2014

Venkatesh, V., Chan, F. K., & Thong, J. Y. (2012). Designing e-government services: Key service attributes and citizens' preference structures. *Journal of Operations Management, 30*(1), 116–133.

Verheijen, T. (2007). Public administration in post-communist states. In B. G. Peters & J. Pierre (Eds.), *Handbook of public administration* (pp. 311–319). London: SAGE Publications Ltd.

Wang, X., & Wan Wart, M. (2007). When public participation in administration leads to trust: An empirical assessment of managers' perceptions. *Public Administration Review, 67*(2), 265–278.

Warf, B. (2013). The Central Asian digital divide. In M. Ragnedda & G. Muschert (Eds.), *The digital divide: The Internet and social inequality in international perspective* (pp. 270–281). London and New York: Routledge.

Welsh, H. A. (1996). Dealing with the communist past: Central and East European experiences after 1990. *Europe-Asia Studies, 48*(3), 413–428.

West, D. (2007). Global e-government, 2007. http://www.insidepolitics.org/egovt07int.pdf

The World Bank (2016). The Ease of Doing Business in Kazakhstan. http://www.doingbusiness.org/data/exploreeconomies/kazakhstan

Yin, R. K. (2013). *Case study research: Design and methods.* Thousand Oaks, CA: Sage Publications.

Zerde (2015). The National Telecommunication Holding. www.zerde.gov.kz

The Zhilstroysberbank Project (2015). www.hcsbk.kz

Index